"The war of the sexes is historical, and methods of creating peace are plentiful, but few work well. In *The Women's Guide to How Men Think*, the author, a man, offers women a code to male thinking that could bring an end to this war, if embraced. Readable, practical, and wise, I recommend this book to all women who want to understand men and to all men who would like a better understanding of themselves."

—**Harville Hendrix, PhD**, author of *Getting the Love You Want* and coauthor of *Making Marriage Simple*

"Shawn Smith's book is not only notable for its helpful contents, but also for the way in which he opens his heart and mind as an authentic, personal ambassador of the good men he represents. In every chapter he gently but firmly builds upon his basic premises: women can master the tools to get more of what they need from their men, guys are relatively easy to love if women don't expect them to be like them, and women and men need each other's core contributions if they want to create the ultimate fulfillment each of them deserves. In a unique blend of substantial research, humor, and a strong conviction in what he believes in, Smith delivers his story in a manner that is easy to embrace."

—**Randi Gunther, PhD**, author of *Relationship Saboteurs*

"We have always known that men and women think differently, and now that difference is brought to light in an uplifting, easy-to-read guide to understanding how the male mind actually works. Smith has given women the gift of how to really get to know the man they love, and how to love him more."

—**Barton Goldsmith, PhD**, author of *The Happy Couple*

"Shawn Smith has written a powerful primer for modern women who have not been schooled in gender differences. *The Woman's Guide to How Men Think* takes a gentle approach to helping women understand what makes men tick—which will, in turn, help women find the love they seek."

—**Suzanne Venker**, author and cultural critic

"Shawn Smith's book provides a wonderful service in helping women understand men. He weaves together research, clinical experience, and personal experience in a clear, accessible way. I will recommend this book to clients and students, as he is able to highlight the influence of gender without stereotyping or being simplistic. Smith shows us how to avoid the trap of resentment that comes with misunderstanding, and gives thoughtful and practical examples that can improve relationships."

—**Shelly Smith-Acuña, PhD**, author of *Systems Theory in Action* and dean of the graduate school of professional psychology at the University of Denver

"I can't think of another self-help book I've enjoyed reading so much. It's rare to find one that is not only scientifically-based and incredibly practical, but also laced with humor. Chocablock full of fascinating insights into male psychology, this book provides an honest, realistic, and effective pathway for improving and enriching your closest relationships."

—**Russ Harris**, author of *The Happiness Trap*

"Shawn Smith does not apologize for male traits, nor does he try to change them. Instead, he reveals what they mean to women who want a better relationship with the man who possesses those traits. This book walks female readers through the male mind, and helps them understand how to be more empathetic and connected to the man they love. This book teaches that men's behavior and love is not better or worse, just different. Acknowledging the difference is what makes this guide a gem."

—**Helen Smith, PhD**, author of *Men on Strike: Why Men Are Boycotting Marriage, Fatherhood, and the American Dream—and Why It Matters* and forensic psychologist in Knoxville, TN

"Smith is a brilliant writer who explains the mysteries of the male mind with intelligence, compassion, and humor. His well-researched book is a compelling guide that provides a better understanding of men and will result in improved relationships. This is a must-read for every woman."

—**Michelle Skeen, PsyD**, radio show host and author of *The Critical Partner*

"A thoroughly enjoyable read! This book is an easy and practical guide for those looking to understand some of the key aspects of the male mind. With relevant research, interesting case studies, and easy-to-follow man tips, this book makes men more accessible in relationships. It sheds light on why men crave being effective, and the way they differ in terms of problem solving, listening, and needing appreciation. It also highlights common male patterns like the 'silence hole' and offers ways to get men to be more present and engaged. Reading this book will give you a new perspective on the man in your life."

—**John Aiken**, relationship psychologist, TV host, and best-selling author

"If you are lost in translation when you are trying to communicate with your man, this is the go-to guide for you. Smith provides a wonderfully clear understanding of the relational disconnect that plagues many relationships. In reader-friendly language, he presents sound and positive strategies to help struggling couples. It is an invaluable resource!"

—**Carolyn Daitch, PhD**, author of *Anxious in Love*

"At first glance, *A Woman's Guide to How Men Think* suggests a twenty-first century version of John Gray's classic, *Men are from Mars, Women are from Venus*; however, rather than focus on men at their worst, Shawn Smith writes about what he terms 'good men.' As a therapist who promotes secure-functioning relationships, I find his premise—that there are men willing and able to love and commit in relationships—refreshing. Readers of both genders should find this book sheds new light on many of the age-old dilemmas of pair bonding."

—**Stan Tatkin, PsyD, MFT**

The Woman's Guide

to

How Men Think

Love,
Commitment,
and the
Male Mind

SHAWN T. SMITH, PsyD

New Harbinger Publications, Inc.

Publisher's Note

This publication is designed to provide accurate and authoritative information in regard to the subject matter covered. It is sold with the understanding that the publisher is not engaged in rendering psychological, financial, legal, or other professional services. If expert assistance or counseling is needed, the services of a competent professional should be sought.

Distributed in Canada by Raincoast Books

Copyright © 2013 by Shawn Smith
New Harbinger Publications, Inc.
5674 Shattuck Avenue
Oakland, CA 94609
www.newharbinger.com

Cover design by Amy Shoup; Text design by Tracy Marie Carlson
Acquired by Melissa Kirk; Edited by Jasmine Star

Library of Congress Cataloging-in-Publication Data

Smith, Shawn T., 1967-
  The woman's guide to how men think : love, commitment, and the male mind / Shawn T. Smith, PsyD.
      pages cm
  Includes bibliographical references.
  ISBN 978-1-60882-789-3 (pbk. : alk. paper) -- ISBN 978-1-60882-790-9 (pdf e-book) -- ISBN 978-1-60882-791-6 (epub) 1. Man woman relationships--Psychological aspects. 2. Men--Psychology. 3. Sex differences (Psychology) 4. Couples--Psychology. I. Title.
  HQ801.S656 2014
  155.3'32--dc23
                                               2013041599

Printed in the United States of America

15   14   13

10   9   8   7   6   5   4   3   2   1   First printing

Contents

Part 3
How to Speak Manese

Acknowledgments

These few words of gratitude are insufficient for all the help and support others have contributed to this book. My everlasting thanks go to Melissa Kirk and all of the wonderful professionals at New Harbinger for bringing this book to life, and to Jasmine Star for her flawless editing. To the hundreds of men and women who anonymously shared their thoughts as this book was taking shape, thank you for your wisdom. Special gratitude goes to friends who endured the first draft and offered invaluable feedback: Russ Harris, Veronica Hoegler, Jonathan Lipson, Stephanie Marsh, Michelle Skeen, and Valerie Wickwar-Svoboda. And most of all, my love and gratitude to Tracy and Jordan. Without you, my life and my work would be meaningless.

Introduction

I knew a man—let's call him Mike—who unintentionally caused his wife a great deal of angst. He meant well, but sometimes good intentions can have bad results.

The problem began on a random Tuesday afternoon when Mike learned that his employer might soon be reducing its workforce. Being one of the newer employees, he worried that his job was in jeopardy.

Mike confided in a friend but otherwise kept his concerns to himself. He didn't tell his wife, Amy, about his fears. Instead, he started looking for a new job in the hopes that he would find something before he lost his current job. He wanted to spare Amy from worrying about their income.

You can probably guess what happened. Mike lost his job and hid it from Amy. When she thought he was at work, he was actually *looking* for work. He also spent a fair portion of his days at bars trying to drown his anxiety.

Amy suspected a problem because Mike seemed preoccupied, and she was beginning to notice the smell of alcohol on his breath during the workweek. She finally pressed him for answers after she received a warning that their car payment was overdue.

Only then did Mike finally admit the truth to Amy. He hadn't earned a paycheck in weeks, and they were beginning to fall behind on their bills.

Amy was angry, but for reasons Mike didn't expect or completely understand. His focus had been on keeping them financially afloat and protecting Amy from anxiety. Her concern, on the other hand, was for their relationship.

From her point of view, their money problem was transient, but their relationship was irreplaceable. Mike should have trusted her enough to confide in her. Besides, she told him, she could have easily helped with the financial shortfall if he had given her some warning. His defense was that he was just trying to be a good provider.

Mike stomped out of the house that night before the conversation was over. He appeared angry, but inside—and for reasons he couldn't quite articulate at the time—he felt wounded.

This type of situation can cause a relationship to dissolve, but don't worry about Mike and Amy. Their story has a happy ending, and I'll come back to it shortly.

A Book About Good Men

What causes a well-intentioned man like Mike to disengage from the relationship when there's a problem, rather than turning to his partner for help? And for that matter, what causes men to be so competitive with each other, make fools of themselves trying to impress women, turn into depressed couch potatoes after a few years of marriage, or do any of the other seemingly inexplicable things they do in relationships? What the heck is going on inside the male mind?

This book is for anyone who's is interested in how men operate in relationships. Chances are, you're reading this book with a particular man in mind—one you'd like to understand better. You may be wondering if this book will be useful. Will it really help you improve your relationship?

There's an inherent problem in books like this. The man you might be thinking of is a unique individual, not a statistical average. It's like buying a book called *How Cars Work* when you're trying to maintain a 1972 Lamborghini Miura.

Okay, maybe your man isn't that racy, but you get my point (and kudos if you can pick a Miura out of a lineup). The man you're thinking of is an individual, and I'm offering generalizations.

Generalizations are uncomfortable, and for good reason. As I was writing this book, hundreds of men and women participated in a survey in which I asked for their thoughts about the genders. A few people felt compelled to begin their responses with "I don't like to generalize, but…"

There's wisdom in that hesitance. In relationships, particulars are more important than generalities. Imagine a woman saying to her husband, "Honey, I don't understand why you're struggling with erectile dysfunction. Most men don't have that problem."

Can you think of a more efficient way to aggravate the situation? I can't. That's the problem with generalizations. They don't apply neatly to individuals, and they can make things worse. That's why every generalization in a book like this matters less than individual traits. Most men like cars, but that's irrelevant if your man doesn't.

Still, some generalizations are valid and useful. For example, men and women possess different levels of androgens (often called male hormones). Those hormone levels affect things like mechanical aptitude, mood, cardiovascular efficiency, speed, endurance, muscle mass, aggressiveness, and the tendency to scratch oneself in public. While this doesn't mean that, for example, some women aren't stronger than some men, it does belie the hippie-trippy 1960s notion that the brains of men and women are identical.

That brings me to the second reason that generalizations can be uncomfortable: acknowledging differences invokes the fear that one gender is superior to the other. I imagine that's one reason so many people endorse the old idea that men and women are essentially identical. If men are stronger, maybe that means men are better. If women are more empathetic, maybe that means they're superior to men.

Not in this book. I believe it's most accurate and useful to think of men and women as different but equal, with strengths and weaknesses that are wonderfully, perfectly complementary.

Here's my stance, which also happens to be the stance put forth by evolutionary psychology: male and female bodies are nearly identical, except for the differences that arose out of distinct reproductive tasks. The same is true of our minds. They are essentially the same except where we differ because of our respective reproductive tasks, our distinct physical abilities, and the need for the genders to relate to each other. Not better, not worse, just different.

Those differences, to my occasionally romantic mind, are wondrous. They are to be celebrated. I believe they make life worth living.

Now that you know where I stand, let the generalizations begin! The first and most important generalization is that this is a book about *good* men. I'm particular about that term. The drives and thinking patterns I'll discuss apply to mature men who mostly have their act together.

That's not to say that all good men think alike, but they do share some basic characteristics, such as the desire to care for those around them or to be as effective as possible in professional endeavors.

Men who are immature or of low character—as well as otherwise good men who are momentarily failing to conduct themselves in a respectable manner—face a different set of challenges. Little of this book will apply to men who are abusive, addicted, dishonest, or tethered to a game console in their mother's basement. Those aren't necessarily bad men, but I won't be discussing them. I'll focus on a higher level of male motivation and thinking. If you're hoping to improve your relationship with a good man, this book should offer useful insight.

Who Wrote This Book?

At this point, you might be wondering who the heck am I to write a book about good men. I was a typical boy with typical struggles. As a kid, I liked to climb trees and play with fire. My friends and I would build things, knock them down, and then build them again. I was energetic and distracted, and I had problems with authority. I was lucky enough to spend my formative years hauling beer, washing dishes, and scrubbing floors in my father's bar. There, I witnessed grown men doing good things, as well as bad.

All these years later, I'm a fairly typical man. I can hang drywall, replace brake pads, and wire a three-way switch. My problems with authority remain, and I have typical male struggles in relationships. Just ask my wife.

Oh, and did I mention that I can bench-press a solid sixty pounds? Impressive, no? (Well, maybe I could bench that much if I weren't cursed with the spindly arms of a psychologist.)

Yes, I'm also a clinical psychologist who works with couples and who is fascinated by the ways in which men and women complement and contradict each other. I wrote this book to address some of the common relationship problems related to the ways men think and act around their partners.

If this book improves understanding between the genders and instills a bit of domestic tranquility in a few homes, it will have done its job. As a typical man, I'm always striving to do a good job.

What to Expect

Before I address what to expect, first a few words on what *not* to expect. This book won't offer advice on how to change the nature of a man, nor will it advise you to change your nature to suit him. Neither is necessary. You'll find no apologies for male traits, nor will you find excuses for bad male behavior. (Bad behavior will be an occasional topic because it shouldn't be tolerated, but it is sometimes tricky to recognize.) Instead, I'll focus on creating harmony between the genders, embracing our differences, and enjoying more fulfilling relationships.

Part 1 of the book exposes some of the most important things that drive men. I'll talk about how men think and why they behave the way they do in relationships. Think of it as the "How Cars Work" portion of the book. If you've ever wondered why men do things like abandon the loving arms of their family for the cold demands of the workplace, read on. You'll also find plenty of helpful tips in part 1.

In parts 2 and 3, I get to the real meat and potatoes of improving relationships with men. I'll discuss things like getting men to actually hear you and how to bypass the most common mistakes in communicating with a man.

At the end of most chapters, you'll notice brief sections titled "For the Man in Your Life." I included these sections in case the man in question happens to thumb through this book in search of ways to make life easier, as men are prone to do. If you are a woman, do not, under any circumstance, read these sections.

Ha! Just kidding. Perhaps you'll find them interesting. They might also help you spark conversations about some of the things men rarely discuss with women. In fact, I hope this book will be the source of many good conversations between you and your partner.

There are a couple of other things to expect.

The first relates to the aforementioned unscientific survey I conducted while writing this book. I used the Internet to ask women what they wish they understood about men, and to ask men what they wish women understood about them.

Somewhat to my surprise, hundreds of men answered my questions, and even more women participated. You'll find their thoughts throughout the book. Some are complimentary and some are critical, but all of them are undiluted and straight from the source.

Second, I'll share the stories of several couples throughout the book. I chose their stories because their problems, strengths, and relationship patterns are typical of the things that come up when someone decides to date or marry a good man. And speaking of those case studies...

What Happened to Mike and Amy?

When we left Mike and Amy, he had marched out of the house in midconversation. Mike felt wounded but didn't know why, and Amy felt discouraged about the relationship because it seemed as though Mike didn't love her enough to confide in her and seek her help.

I chose their story because Mike's male nature—his *good* male nature—was the source of their difficulty. He simply wanted to be an effective partner. He didn't want to feel diminished in Amy's eyes. That's why he hid the problem from her.

Mike and Amy didn't let this problem ruin their relationship. Instead, they did a couple of things to avoid similar problems in the future. First, they developed a deeper understanding of their individual traits. Amy didn't quite understand Mike's need to feel pride in himself, but she accepted that it was terribly important to him. And Mike gained a new understanding of how badly his withdrawal hurt Amy.

Second, they improved their ability to recognize the true nature of their emotional reactions. Mike appeared angry when he left the house that night. He even said that he was angry. But beneath that veneer of anger he felt great shame at his inability to, in his view, properly care for his partner. (This is one of the things you should know about us: our man-hood must be earned and constantly maintained, and our man-card is always subject to revocation if we stop performing our duties.)

That sense of duty—that need to be useful—is one of the first things this book looks at. Many men have told me that this is one of the things that women seem to have a hard time understanding about them, and it causes a slew of problems between the genders.

But that's just the beginning. We have a lot of ground to cover, so pull up a comfy old recliner, crack a beer, and let's take a look inside the male mind.

Part 1

A Day in the Life
of a Male Mind

Good men are dutiful men. They want to be effective in their lives, their careers, and their relationships. They are driven to be devoted and capable, and a good man wants to be the most important thing in the world to the woman in his life.

Unfortunately, people's greatest strengths often hold the seeds of their deepest struggles, and that's certainly true of the good and dutiful man. His need to be effective skews the way he views himself, his partner, and his relationship. It can even be a destructive force when he finds his loyalties overburdened outside of the relationship, or when expectations change within it.

Despite its perils, that need for effectiveness remains an ancient and powerful force for good. It shapes men profoundly, and it is one of the most important things to understand about good and dutiful men.

Chapter 1

The Most Important Thing to Men

Lack of purpose is a terrible thing for the male mind. Why do unemployed men get depressed, young men join street gangs, and unmarried men die sooner? In my estimation, it's at least partly because they lack purpose. Good men are a bit like border collies: we're happiest when we're useful. That's why the life of a good man involves constant striving for direction and meaning.

We men can find our purpose in many places—work, play, camaraderie with other men—but nothing scratches that itch quite like devoting ourselves to a good woman. Sure, sometimes we carp about the women in our lives, but even our complaining is evidence of our drive to be committed to something larger than ourselves. Here's an example of what I mean: "Women assume that we know what's wrong and how to fix it, when 99 percent of the time we're utterly clueless and they won't tell us. And then when we finally figure out what's wrong, they don't want our help, which leaves us feeling completely powerless to make them happy."

(That's a response to the survey I told you about. How about this: just assume that future quotes came from the survey unless I attribute them to someone in particular. Deal?)

At first glance, the man who wrote that may appear to be frustrated or angry. But really, he probably just wants to know what women want. Like so many guys, he's looking for a way to fulfill his purpose in her world. The need for purpose is at the core of our male selves.

Maybe you've heard the joke about the woman who worried about the future until she found a husband, and the man who never worried about the future until he found a wife. It comes from the old stereotype that women want to pin a man down, while men simply want to carouse and enjoy the company of as many women as possible.

Even science-minded people like evolutionary psychologists are tempted to imagine early men on the savanna philandering about like hairy, Stone Age Casanovas, while cunning women tried to wile or coerce them into monogamy for the safety of their children.

There may be a grain of truth to the philandering stereotype. DNA evidence suggests that, long ago, women outnumbered men by about two to one. That was probably the most effective breeding ratio at that point in history (Wilder, Mobasher, and Hammer 2004). The same evidence suggests that most women had babies, which means there must have been a bit of polygyny (the technical term for multiple wives) in Fred Flintstone's day.

That doesn't mean that men didn't love and commit themselves to individual women. The idea that men avoid committed, long-term relationships, either then or now, seems to be quite incorrect.

Research into the history of mating suggests that men desire lifelong mates as much as women do (Buss 1998). Historically, men may have had a penchant to care for more than one woman at a time, but still, men and women are much more similar than different in their desire for romantic stability.

By necessity, men and women pursue committed relationships in different ways. For example, several decades' worth of research shows that, across cultures, men tend to focus on physical attractiveness in a mate more than women do, while women place more importance on good financial prospects in a man (Shackelford, Schmitt, and Buss 2005).

That probably isn't a news flash, but it is the kind of thing that drives men to behave in ways that don't always add up for women. Why? Because we men are aware that you look for many different qualities in us: emotional stability, kindness, intelligence, and so on, and we can trip over our own intentions while trying to impress you.

We are also painfully aware that, even though there are plenty of women who don't place a premium on a man's resources, men with higher resources have always been more successful in the mating game. That isn't a moral reflection on either gender; it's simply a historical truth, and men closely monitor these truths.

What does something like that do to a man's mind? For starters, it may help explain why male nature is so competitive. Most of us are driven to work harder, get more, and be better than the competition. That is what you want, right?

Of course, that isn't always what you want, but that's what we *think* you want, and we're always trying to be useful to you. Unfortunately, our innate desire to be competitive, useful, and worthy of your love sometimes causes us to do the least useful and most unlovable things. That's what happened to Sam.

• Sam and Tamara

Sam had always been the good kid who did the right things. He earned good grades in high school, went to the right college, and always kept the tires properly inflated, just as his father had taught him.

At twenty-eight, he married his longtime girlfriend, Tamara. His career was on track, and he even became one of his company's youngest managers. He was becoming a devoted employee and family man. Tamara found his stability and ambition wonderfully attractive.

They embarked on their marriage well, using premarital counseling to help them negotiate their spousal roles before tying the knot. As it turned out, they both wanted a traditional arrangement. Sam would work, and Tamara would stay home with the kids. Because Sam did well financially, they had that option, which few couples can afford these days. Two years into their marriage, Tamara happily set aside her career as a physical therapist to prepare for the birth of their first child.

Things went well for a while. But like many new parents, they were surprised at the amount of work involved in child rearing. They hadn't anticipated the sleep deprivation and the loss of personal time.

At the same time, Sam's job was becoming more demanding and time-consuming. Due to the stress at work and at home, small resentments began to mount between Sam and Tamara.

Evening rituals were one of their points of contention. By the time Sam got home from work in the evenings, Tamara was exhausted and anticipated that he'd take over the child care for the rest of the night. At the same time, the demands of Sam's job were taking an increasingly high toll. He often came home from long and stressful workdays so exhausted that he was ineffective and impatient with their son, Jake.

Sam felt he was in a double bind. He knew Tamara needed his help and he wanted to do the best he could, but tensions were rising, and he sensed that Tamara was increasingly disappointed in him. He also knew that he couldn't allow his work to suffer because that would harm their income, adding even more pressure at home. He needed his job to maintain their stability.

In a sense, his family was becoming a threat to the job that provided their food and shelter, while his job was becoming a threat to the family that made the job necessary.

In situations like this, men can become binary in their logic: if two situations are mutually exclusive, they attend to the most pressing one. Sam thought he had to choose between making his employer angry or making his wife angry. He figured that his family could survive an angry wife more easily than it could survive an angry employer.

Indeed, Tamara was becoming angry. She began to criticize Sam about being unavailable. She was concerned that Jake wouldn't know his father. She was lonely, and she wanted a partner rather than someone who simply provided a paycheck.

Sam reacted to Tamara's frustration by avoiding arguments, like a kid who exacerbates a bad report card by hiding it. To avoid conflict with Tamara, he spent more time at work because that at least added to their income. He fantasized that more money would ease Tamara's unhappiness.

Sam's biggest mistake—one that's common among good men—was hiding his problem from Tamara, and everyone else, because he thought talking about it seemed whiny: *I'm a man, dammit. I got us into this, and I'll get us out.* He began putting more time and effort into his job with the hope that soon he'd achieve a level of success that would allow him to maintain his income level and also spend more time at home.

It was a naive wish. As Sam invested more time in his work, his job demanded more of him, so he spent even less time at home. And as Tamara became increasingly unhappy, his job became an escape from a home environment where he felt ineffective and unappreciated. Privately, he wondered if committing himself to work was the right decision, but he stayed the course. He didn't want to act with indecision or ambivalence.

While Sam had given his family plenty of security, they were anything but happy. Tamara wondered where her good and responsible husband had gone, while Sam became increasingly resentful that Tamara didn't appreciate his hard work and devotion.

"I Am My Responsibilities"

What would cause a responsible man like Sam to abandon a tight-knit family for the cold, hard workplace? The short answer is that he felt he had to balance two mutually exclusive tasks. He believed he couldn't keep both his wife and his boss happy, so he made a pragmatic choice that he thought would cause the least damage.

But that perspective was skewed. In fact, it was a bit self-serving. Sam got to *feel* as if he was being a dutiful man when in fact his sense of duty was causing him to ignore the people he had pledged to serve.

The problem started when Sam decided to shoulder the burden with manly stoicism. He acted on instinct, and instinct told him to work harder. That made his boss happy, and Sam got the satisfaction of doing something that would benefit his family, even though he had a nagging sense of uncertainty about whether it was the best course. Good men are prone to this variety of shortsightedness.

His decision may have been influenced by the fact that men come equipped with a team mentality and an orientation toward duty. Our workmates are important because they are tied to our survival, so if we're pressed, we sometimes give them precedence over other people, including family members. This strange bit of male logic is not without merit. By devoting ourselves to that which provides resources, we're indirectly devoting ourselves to the ones we love because we're advancing their survival too.

Whether or not it's perfectly logical, this seems to be inborn in men. Research suggests that men have more of an innate team mentality than women. For example, men cooperate more than women when their group is in competition with other groups. Cooperation between women, on the other hand, is mostly unaffected by intergroup competition (Van Vugt, De Cremer, and Janssen 2007). Researchers have even discovered that a pheromone in male sweat increases cooperation between men, and contrary to what one might expect, so does a high testosterone level (Huoviala and Rantala 2013).

None of this suggests that women don't cooperate, but men seem to be wired to meet difficult challenges as a team—except for air guitar and hot-dog–eating contests, which are strictly individual sports. (I'll revisit the topic of male teamwork and how it affects intimate relationships in chapter 4.)

When a man like Sam has to make a choice between fulfilling a duty to an individual (in this case, his wife) and the team that exists in his workplace, it isn't always an easy decision. Rather than being pulled toward intimacy, Sam felt pulled toward a solution that eliminated the largest number of problems. By devoting himself to people outside the home, he could accomplish several things at once:

* Maintaining his good standing within his work team and increasing his family's security

* Satisfying his duty to his family by bringing home the bacon

* Reducing conflict with his wife by staying out of her way

* Acting as an effective man by doing what he's good at

Most men are aware of the trade-offs, even if they don't like them. In his attempt to find the most effective and efficient solution, Sam distanced himself from his wife and son. Men in Sam's position often feel as if they're facing a cold emotional equation in which being decisive and effective is bound to make someone unhappy. Whether that's true or just his mistaken perception, it can become a heavy burden.

Putting Words to the Problem

One of Sam's mistakes was his failure to consider alternatives. Good men often have to prioritize duties, but we sometimes lack the insight to make the best choice for ourselves or those to whom we are duty bound. In part, that's due to the fact that we often don't put words to our struggles. Masculine stoicism keeps us from doing so, and that keeps us from recognizing our alternatives.

Paul Giblin, PhD, a researcher into marriage and the spirituality of men, notes that men struggle more than women to connect words to their internal experiences, and also struggle with understanding and applying their thoughts, feelings, and values about commitment (2011). Many of us, like Sam, simply aren't practiced at resolving emotional conflicts.

Giblin found that men commonly feel deep regret after making a commitment or feel constrained to commitments they wish they hadn't made. This is often because we don't label and think about our emotions before we make decisions.

It is not for me to say whether Sam made the wrong decision, but I believe that he lost track of his alternatives, and that deciding unilaterally to increasingly focus on work was unfair to Tamara. Deep down, Sam realized that he was aggravating the problem, but stoicism prevented him from seeking the middle ground that could have satisfied both Tamara and his employer.

In addition, Sam's sense of responsibility complicated things. If you ask any good man for his definition of manhood, he's likely to use the word "responsibility" somewhere in his answer. We view ourselves in large measure as members of groups that have jobs to do, and many of us become overextended in our commitments. Responsibility and service are the lifeblood of good men, but as Sam could attest, the desire to be responsible can impair foresight.

"I Am My Status"

One woman who completed my online survey said she didn't understand "the unwritten body language between men that seems to quickly establish a man's rank within the pack." She didn't understand how we so quickly "take the measure of a man's worth," nor did she grasp our desire to compete for the position of top dog.

Despite not understanding these male behaviors, her observations were correct. We do compete and compare. Seeking and measuring status seems to be a lifelong pursuit of the male gender, from peewee football to the workplace and beyond. For men, life can feel like a never-ending job interview.

Sometimes we make it easy to judge status, for example, displaying rank and decorations on military uniforms. (Women wear uniforms too, but that's a relatively recent development in human history.) But even without markers of rank, we are quite sophisticated in judging our status relative to other men.

This assessment of rank even takes context into account. The same man may be more dominant in one setting and more submissive in another. We can

> ## How Men Think
>
> **"I think women have a hard time understanding what drives men to work as hard as we do. My motivation is a yearning to leave a legacy."**

switch roles without missing a beat when the context calls for it. And those who stand to lose the most in a contest of dominance are most attentive and sensitive to status (Watkins and Jones 2012).

Men also respond to both physical and social dominance in a similar way, despite the fact that these are quite different things (Watkins and Jones 2012). That gives us the ability to establish dominance without violence, since losing an argument affects our perception of dominance the same as losing a fight. Men who have recently lost in nonviolent social conflicts are more sensitive to dominance cues from other men. This illustrates how important hierarchy is in the lives of men, and it's just one set of behaviors that help us peacefully establish a pecking order.

That's not all. We also closely watch contests between other men. We're constantly judging ourselves and recalibrating our position, which may be why we seem to obsess about status. One of the great advantages to our constant, internal recalibration is the degree to which it reduces conflict. When each man in a group continuously monitors his own status and performance, others don't have to keep him in line. Anyone who claims that men don't cooperate hasn't watched us very closely.

Still, the question remains: Why are men so concerned with status?

The overly simple answer, which holds some truth, is that high-status men are more attractive to women. Even adolescent boys who join gangs (one of the quickest ways to achieve status) are judged to be more attractive by adolescent girls and have more sexual partners than their nongang counterparts (Palmer and Tilly 1995).

To a large degree, status matters to men because it matters to women, which researchers have demonstrated in a carefully controlled experiment (Guéguen and Lamy 2012). To test the idea, they placed men in expensive cars and instructed them to approach women and ask for their phone number. Then they had the men do the same thing in medium- and low-status cars.

The results? The men were successful 23.3 percent of the time when women saw them in a high-status car, 12.8 percent of the time when they drove a middle-status car, and 7.8 percent of the time when they drove a low-status car. Clearly, women are monitoring our status, and we're acutely aware of that fact.

But impressing women is just part of the reason for our obsession with status. Awareness of status also helps us stay in good graces with other men. Status is an extension of our duty and plays a role in defining it. Our concern over status also reduces conflict, increases efficiency, and makes men more cooperative with each other (McIntyre et al. 2011).

Male status seeking can be a source of frustration for women who find it challenging to live with, or who don't need their men to be millionaires or presidents. But our status-seeking behavior keeps us on good terms with other men, and with women, because it forces us to monitor our own behavior. If our concern over status is annoying or frustrating, just imagine how we might act without it.

The Importance of Being Effective

When Sam experienced a problem in his relationship with his wife, he pulled away from her. He retreated into his job. You might say this wasn't a masculine thing to do. Good men should face up to their problems, shouldn't they?

People *should* do lots of things. But when stressed, people turn to their old, reliable strategies. With men, that sometimes means relying on the status and responsibility strategies with which we are most comfortable. People like to do what they know best.

Suppose a company was floundering and on the verge of failure. A marketing person would tend to blame the company's problem on poor marketing. An accountant would see the company's accounting problems,

How Men Think

"I don't think women can ever fully understand our need to be useful."

and a manager would see poor management. If people don't force themselves to step back and view the entire system, they'll define problems in terms of what they know.

When Sam—a good and dutiful man—experienced problems in his marriage, he didn't step back and examine the systemic problem. He was vaguely aware of the fact that the harder he worked, the angrier Tamara became. But he hoped that if he could just get over the hump, everything would be okay. Unfortunately, it was as if he was fighting against quicksand. As the relationship became increasingly uncomfortable, he felt increasingly compelled to use his reliable old status and responsibility strategies, and that only made things worse.

Sam's problems began with something that I'll be discussing quite a bit: his need to be effective. He wanted to be the most important thing in the world to his wife and family, which makes it all the more sad and ironic that his strategy created discord.

Sam's need to be effective is typical of good men. Here's what a few men had to say on the topic:

* "We love to help you! We really do. That's what makes us trust our manly worthiness. Your wishes are our commands. We love it when you depend on us."

* "When a woman is proud of you for doing something well, it's a wonderful feeling. I don't mind working twelve hours a day, but like a good dog, I appreciate a scratch and a 'good boy' at the end. ... It sometimes annoys me how much I still want my wife's approval, even though I'm successful at work and in other areas."

* "What do I like most? The way she looks at me when she's impressed by something I've done or said."

Even a seventeen-year-old who responded to my survey had the itch to be useful and effective (though he may need to polish his rough, paternalistic edge): "I like girls who I think need protection, whom I can take care of." A sense of purpose is vital to good men. The downside is that a lot of men frequently seek reassurance about their effectiveness. We fish for compliments, and sometimes this can be annoying. Here's how one woman put it: "Why do men need so much stroking? Isn't a simple 'Thank you, that was great' sufficient? Why do we need to get out the pom-poms and cheer for the slightest little chore accomplished? Come on! It gets tedious!"

Why do we crave appreciation? Because we live to be useful to you. We want to be effective. Good men seem to understand that we are nothing without women. That's why we compete for your attention. That's why we work so hard. That's why effectiveness is the most important thing. And that's why men like Sam can fall headlong into the effectiveness trap. It's tough to find sympathy for Sam at first glance because he created his own problems. Rather than communicating, he retreated. He put his workplace ahead of his family. He made unilateral decisions. In short, he stumbled into the dark side of the male drive for effectiveness.

Make Sure He Has a Way to Win

One of the most common complaints I hear from men whose relationships are in serious trouble is "I can't win with her. I'm damned if I do and damned if I don't."

When men reach the point where they feel that there's no way to be effective in a relationship, where anything and everything they do will create a bad outcome, they often stop trying. Once that apathy sets in, it can be difficult to repair the relationship.

It's easy for couples to fall into this trap. One woman routinely complained that her husband didn't talk to her often enough. But he explained that when he tried to converse with her, she often seized upon it as an opportunity to criticize his behavior. It seemed to him as if he was in trouble when he did speak to his wife, and also in trouble when he didn't speak to her. Ultimately, the relationship didn't last.

If the man in your life begins to complain that there's no way for him to win, heed the warning. (I'll discuss what to do about it in chapter 9.) When he no longer feels that he can be effective in the relationship, he might give up. Don't let that happen. Make sure your man has a way to please you, and make sure he knows what it is.

It's All About You

I began this book with the topics of responsibility, status, and duty because they are so often the source of problems in relationships. Good men need purpose, and that's why women are so important to us. A good man wants to be the most important thing in the world to his mate, and his devotion isn't just about sex.

You're probably thinking, *Really?*

Really. Read on.

For the Man in Your Life:
What Happened to the Woman You Love?

I've heard a lot of men complain that their wives or girlfriends have turned into constant complainers. "No matter what I do," these guys say, "she's never happy. When did she become such a nag?"

This chapter began with the story of Sam, a married man who found himself in a position in which he felt he had to choose between work and family. His job was demanding, and his wife, Tamara, became increasingly unhappy in the first few years of their marriage.

As tensions mounted at home, Tamara complained more and more that Sam wasn't the husband she'd expected him to be. She said that he'd gone back on his promise to be an involved partner and a parent. Sam's defense was that he was simply being a good provider, and in fact he was bringing home a nice paycheck. He wondered how Tamara could complain when he was working so hard to provide for the family.

In truth, Sam was having difficulty striking a balance between work and family. He erred on the side of taking care of his family's financial needs while neglecting their emotional needs. He had good intentions, but he was violating his promise to be present as a partner and a father.

Men in Sam's position frequently fail to ask for help. They try to man up and fix problems on their own, which can sometimes make the situation worse.

In this chapter, I advised women not to put men in no-win situations. For example, Sam's wife was unhappy when he wasn't home and was critical when he was home. No matter what he did, he was in trouble. Men often complain that women too often rely on punishment rather than positive reinforcement.

But positive reinforcement only works when we actually deliver. When we break our promises, as Sam broke his promise to be present for his family, we put women in the position of being our mothers. Of course that's going to make a woman unhappy.

Sam could have avoided a world of heartache if he had simply talked to his wife about his difficulty in balancing his responsibilities. Instead, he soldiered on alone, devoting himself to bringing home a bigger paycheck in the belief that this would fix their problems. As it turns out, he chose poorly. Tamara wanted *him*, not more money, and she gladly would have made lifestyle changes to achieve that.

Don't make Sam's mistake and avoid talking with your partner about problems. That's bound to leave you, like Sam, wondering what happened to the happy woman you fell in love with. It is often a sign of strength, not weakness, to communicate about your concerns and listen to loved ones.

Chapter 2

How Men View Women

A good man wants to be effective. That doesn't necessarily mean he wants to be president; it just means that wherever his values lie—whatever is most important to him—he wants to know that he's the man for the job.

We view ourselves in terms of how useful we are. This means we need someone to serve, and guess what: that's you. To a large degree, we view women in terms of how we can make their lives better. The women in our lives give us a point of reference for our effectiveness. Working for your affection and approval is in our bones.

One man explained it this way: "We're the expendable half of the species, ladies. We're designed to take down the bad guys, to save the children. We're your weapons, your attack dogs. We're ready to die taking down the threats against you. There isn't much call for this in the twenty-first century, but this is our baggage. We're here to solve your problems, and when you have no need for our upper-body strength, raw courage, or foolish daring, we can be at a loss."

Good men are ready and willing to serve, and we start our training at an early age. It is for good reason that the Boy Scout oath begins with the phrase "On my honor, I will do my best." That's just one of many lessons teaching us to stay physically strong, mentally awake, and morally aware so that we can serve others.

Any man who strives to be good and decent will come up short occasionally. Sam, in chapter 1, made one of the classic male mistakes: deciding what he thought would be an effective and useful way to serve his wife without seeking her opinion. (As you may have noticed, in many men's minds being competent and effective means never having to ask for direction—or directions.)

This can make it seem as if we men don't have much going on between our ears or don't know or care about what's going on around us. But the truth is, good men agonize about effectiveness, and there's quite a bit happening in our heads—not that you would know it from our behavior. A classic example of the male need for effectiveness gone wonky is the silent man. Let's take a look at that.

Can Silence Be an Attempt at Effectiveness?

You might recall from chapter 1 that men often have difficulty putting words to their internal experiences. That was probably no surprise to you, since silence is one of the most common complaints about men. As one woman asked, "Why do men shut down rather than try to communicate or reconnect if there's an issue? Why do they hold in thoughts that are actually important and could be useful to share?"

Beginning in childhood, many of us were simply taught not to communicate. We were told that doing so is effeminate. I'll come back to that shortly. For now, let's look at something much subtler and easily overlooked: our silence often reflects a different style of problem solving.

Most men find disagreements with women to be painful experiences. One man put it this way: "We want all the cards on the table so we can deal with the issue at hand and make you happy again. When you're upset, we're upset, no matter how much we try to hide it."

That last sentence describes one of the most important concepts in this chapter. In my experience, women underestimate the effect that their happiness has on the men in their lives. I'm not suggesting that women should stifle their emotions in order to keep men happy. I'm just pointing out that we're deeply affected by your happiness, even when we don't appear to be.

Most men yearn to be someone who brings happiness and contentment to a woman. Why? The cynical answer is that we're motivated by sex, which we are, but there's much more to it than that.

Yes, We Want to Sleep with You, But...

We've all heard it: men think about sex every seven seconds. I won't be foolish enough to make the case that sex is unimportant to men. I might as well argue that food and water don't matter either. But there's no research to support that seven-second statistic. In fact there's little research into the amount of time that men devote to thoughts of sex. However, a study of college students has revealed a few facts.

On average, men think about sex more frequently than women, but not by a large measure, and some women think about sex more frequently than the average man. A person's openness to sex more accurately predicts the frequency of their sexual thoughts than does their gender (Fisher, Moore, and Pittenger 2012).

Don't misunderstand this red-blooded American man. Sex is important to men, and our minds certainly wander in that direction. But when we're in the midst of balancing a checkbook or landing an airplane, I can assure you that we don't stop to think about gettin' it on.

For some men, sex is about conquest. Most people have encountered an unscrupulous Lothario bent on bedding as many women as possible, but such men are in the minority. If they weren't, few men would get married. We would be too busy seducing women to devote ourselves to staying home and cleaning the gutters.

A romantic relationship is about intimacy, even for men. You might say that sex is how we're intimate with you, and service is how we cherish you. I think that can be difficult for women to grasp because men and women have different ways of expressing affection, and even good men have difficulty being vulnerable enough to express what they think and feel.

The Rule of Stoicism

Cameron Gridley, a couples and sex therapist in Denver, Colorado, explained to me that one of the biggest challenges for men is allowing themselves to be emotionally exposed, which includes talking openly about needs and desires. Here's how many men seem to work: if they expose their emotions, they're displaying weakness and opening themselves to criticism, mocking, or rejection. Most of us have been socialized through painful lessons to believe that emotional vulnerability will lead to rejection. Boys who show emotional vulnerability are often ridiculed or punished by other boys or men.

Those harsh lessons aren't necessarily bad. They teach us to be tough and effective. The downside is that we have difficulty knowing when to drop our guard. We overlearn the lesson and apply it even when it would be useful to make ourselves emotionally available to a caring partner.

And because we can't eliminate emotions altogether, we sometimes hide a "weak" emotion, such as sadness, with a "strong" one, such as anger, or with an action like humor or withdrawal. Cameron Gridley calls that replacement emotion a secondary reaction, a term I'll be using throughout the book. It's like a mask that hides the true feeling. Men are largely unaware of these secondary reactions. We hide our emotions, often even from ourselves because part of the secondary reaction's job is to insulate us from our own pain. One of the great relationship challenges for men is to recognize secondary reactions, avoid getting drawn into them, and instead identify the emotions that lie beneath.

Here's a common example: A man tries to comfort his partner but is ineffective in doing so. As a result, he might become indignant and withdraw. Indignation and withdrawal are his secondary reactions. Inside, he may be feeling hurt and sad about not being able to help his partner feel better. But rather than allowing himself to be vulnerable enough to admit his true feelings, he hides them. In fact, couples often end up arguing over secondary reactions like withdrawal, rather than addressing what's going on in the man's mind.

Here's how one self-aware man explained his withdrawal: "Normally, when I'm not talking it's because I've been hurt or irritated. I have to word things carefully because it's hard to let you know I'm in pain without hurting your feelings."

Cameron Gridley believes that many men find it so intolerable to be emotionally vulnerable that they hide their feelings even in the midst of intimacy and sex. He told me that in his practice, he has found that most men consider sex to be an act of intimacy rather than mere physical pleasure, but the pressure to perform and the risk of being emotionally vulnerable can ruin that intimacy. They wear their mask of stoicism and effectiveness even—perhaps especially—when sharing one of life's most intimate connections.

That emotional distance can leave a woman feeling used and unappreciated when the real culprit may be the rule of male stoicism: if you don't get vulnerable, you won't get hurt.

Why We Need to Impress You

Even during acts of intimacy, men try to impress women. Cameron Gridley believes that many men's desire to be impressive in bed causes them to lose track of their partner's desires. This is just one of many examples of how great men are at getting in their own way. I once saw a young man stand up on his moving motorcycle in an attempt to impress a group of young women. He wrecked both the motorcycle and himself.

Maybe you've seen one of those cartoon diagrams of a man's brain in which most of the brain areas are labeled "sex." Those cartoons might be more accurate if they depicted a man's brain as one giant marketing firm designed to earn the affection and admiration of women.

Impressing you with our effectiveness is so central to our identity that we sometimes lose touch with reality. We can get lost in what we *think* you want rather than finding out what you really want. (Maybe a corollary to the rule of stoicism is that the more we communicate, the more vulnerable we are to discovering that we're doing something wrong.)

Let's take a brief aside to talk about what impresses women. If the studies I've cited so far lead you to believe it's all about money, it isn't. Impressing women usually requires a man to use his brain. Intelligence matters to women. You might not know it by watching the men who show up on daytime talk shows, but women long ago decided that smart is sexy.

According to one study, women are adept at quickly detecting intelligence in men, perhaps by subconsciously monitoring traits like creativity and verbal fluency (Prokosch et al. 2009). Intelligence can signify that a man will be a good provider, and that he possesses good genes. All things being equal, intelligent men are more attractive than men of average or lower intelligence.

I've long said that men would be lost without women, and that everything men do is to earn women's favor and impress them. The movie *Star*

Trek: First Contact backs me up. In it, professor Zefram Chochrane explained why he risked his life inventing the fictional warp drive that changed the course of humanity: "I didn't build this ship to usher in a new era for humanity. You think I want to go to the stars? I don't even like to fly! I built this ship so I could retire to some tropical island filled with naked women." Crass, but instructive. Men are willing to risk life and livelihood to impress women. We're programmed to showcase our intelligence and savvy, and sometimes that means playing the odds, even when the odds are against us.

Doing What We Think You Want

We know that you women are watching us, and we want to impress you. Unfortunately, we think you're only interested in the perfect man. What you actually want is slightly different, according to German researchers. Their study (Baur and Hofmeister 2008) found serious discrepancies between what women find attractive and what men think women find attractive. Men tend to think women are only interested in guys who have it all: physical attractiveness, emotional tenderness, and lots of money.

What the women in that study said they wanted was distinctly different. Only 31 percent of them valued all three things in similar measure. These women wanted it all: attractiveness, tenderness, and wealth. The other 69 percent rated some combination of two of those factors as being most important. The most highly prized male traits were related to the first two factors (attractiveness and tenderness), but not wealth: a sense of humor (which any psychologist will tell you is a mark of intelligence), willingness to spend time with his partner, and a fondness for children. In addition, 29 percent of the women said they strongly disagree that it's important for a man to drive an expensive car, which is an indication of financial success.

Perhaps that last point sheds some light on how men begin to get confused about women's desires. As you'll recall from chapter 1, another study seemingly contradicted this one by showing that women are more receptive to date requests from men driving high-status cars than from men driving old clunkers (Palmer and Tilly 1995).

The contradictory messages that show up in scientific studies are the same contradictions that men must somehow reconcile in real life. Most men probably know that only some women place a premium on a man's monetary success. Unfortunately, we can't easily identify what women want simply by sight. As a result, we seem to be programmed to make ourselves attractive to as many women as possible, which means we must assume that all women will only accept the perfect man.

That puts us in a mental bind that we can spend a lifetime trying to reconcile. This is one of the roots of the male psyche. It's why we act ridiculous when we're trying to win you over, like the young man who stood up on his motorcycle, and why we get so confused and frustrated about expectations after we earn your love.

If you'll allow me to get statistical for a moment, earning the affection of women is all about error management. As discussed in my previous book, *The User's Guide to the Human Mind* (Smith 2011), the mind is good at making the right kind of errors in order to keep us safe. For example, suppose you're hiking through the woods and hear a rustling in the bushes. Your brain will bet that something dangerous is making the sound. You might be wrong, but you'll be wrong in the right direction—the safe direction. Incorrectly betting that the situation is safe could be disastrous. Erring instead on the side of safety increases protective behaviors like freezing or running away.

The male mind plays a similar game of chance when it comes to earning a woman's love and admiration. If you're a man trying to be attractive to women, it's logical to assume that every woman demands a man with good looks, emotional tenderness, and money. After all, nearly a third of the women in the study discussed above admitted that they want a man who has it all, so it makes sense for men to err in that direction.

But it does get confusing for men. By way of example, let's delve deeper into the contradictory messages men receive about wealth and resources. In a different car-related experiment, researchers took photographs of a man in two different cars—an expensive silver Bentley Continental GT and a cheap red Ford Fiesta—and asked women to rate his attractiveness (Dunn and Searle 2010). Women found the man, who was dressed the same in both photos, to be significantly more attractive when in the Bentley than when in the Ford. The researchers also reversed the experiment, photographing a woman in the same two cars and asking men to rate her attractiveness. They rated her equally attractive in both.

This is remarkably confusing for men. The majority of women say that material success doesn't matter, and this is undoubtedly true. At the same time, women consistently judge wealthy men to be more attractive. Once again, men are compelled to reconcile the discrepancy by assuming that women want it all in one glorious package of manly perfection.

> ## How Men Think
>
> "Women seem to assume that we automatically know what they want. We don't. We're not mind readers, and our priorities often aren't the same. If you want something, ask. Chances are good that we'll be happy to oblige. I realize that this is partially societal, that women are trained to be independent of men, but seriously, just do it. We'll all be better off."

That type of contradictory message has a deep effect on the way we view ourselves. We tend to judge ourselves inaccurately, and we typically err on the side of caution. We assume that we don't measure up, and that motivates us to keep trying to increase our appeal.

Take physical attractiveness, for example. Women accurately understand what attracts men (Tovée and Cornelissen 2001). But the German study discussed above, assessing the importance of physical attractiveness, tenderness, and wealth, found that men approach their own physical attractiveness the same way they approach money: even the most muscular assume women want them to be more muscular. It's that same old wiring: we aren't sure what you want from us, so we figure we can never have too much of a good thing.

And even when women express their desires directly, there's a little voice in the male mind that asks, *Really? How can you be so sure that she's being honest? Women hide what they really want. Better try harder.* Our desire to please you, combined with our uncertainty about what you truly want, leaves us with abiding angst that we're never really good enough.

Risky Business

Here's another fact men are acutely aware of, and one that leads to further confusion between the genders: women tend to appreciate risk takers. As one woman put it, "I admire a man's willingness to take risks. If a man has real self-confidence, he exudes it without having to put on a display, and that's very sexy."

But once again, women's desires are complex, and we're programmed to satisfy them as best we can. That makes us risk takers in the beginning of a relationship, when we're trying to impress you, but our risk-taking behavior changes as relationships mature.

Men who aren't in relationships tend to take risks that they think women will admire. Men who are in committed relationships, on the other hand, take fewer risks; and the more committed they are to their partner, the fewer risks they take (Frankenhuis and Karremans 2012).

Why do we take risks? For the same reason we do everything else: in an effort to secure your love—and it works. Men who take more recreational, financial, and social risks tend to have had higher prenatal testosterone exposure (Stenstrom et al. 2010), and as a result, they possess masculine traits that women on average find attractive. Men who take risks, like men who are wealthy, are generally more successful in the mating game (Baker and Maner 2008; Wilson and Daly 1985).

Many women complain that once men have earned their love, they become risk averse. That shift in behavior makes perfect sense from the male viewpoint: When a man is courting a woman, the marketing department kicks into high gear and he takes risks. Once he has her love, he stops doing things that threaten his safety and starts doing things that increase security.

It's said that behind every double standard lies a hidden single standard. The single standard here is men's unending desire to be effective. Being effective in drawing your attention and earning your love means taking risks. Being effective in keeping your love means providing security. Men also naturally become more risk averse as their brains mature—a process that isn't complete until well into their twenties—adding another variable to the decline in risky behavior.

Naturally, there are trade-offs to an increased sense of responsibility and decreased risk taking. Among them is that this shift often leaves women wondering what happened to the cool, adventurous guy they fell in love with.

Our Love Is Different from Yours

In our society, men labor under a bias that keeps us perpetually behind the eight ball: the common notion that the female way of doing relationships is the correct way. As one of my colleagues put it, "The model of emotional health is based on the female model of emotional expression."

Here's how one man described the struggle: "I get a lot of grief for not communicating better, even though I have good intentions. Men are always told we need to communicate better. What do women need to do better? Nothing, it seems. Always, the fault seems to be mine. Can a woman lift as much weight as a man? In general, no, and who expects her to? A man would be a jerk for suggesting that she should. Why then are men constantly expected to communicate the same way women do?"

This man isn't alone in his frustration. He has put words to something that countless men face. We've been taught by talk-show hosts, comedians, television commercials, sitcoms, and the women in our lives that relationship problems almost always stem from male behavior. We're told in a thousand different ways that we love you incorrectly.

I think there's a more useful way to look at male relationship behavior: It's simply different. Not better, not worse, just different. Men are prone to demonstrate their love with action rather than through words, as this man explains: "We communicate through our actions more than anything. Women tend to make a big deal out of even the smallest wrongly said thing, but they should really focus on actions. I don't get how failing to comment on a haircut overshadows something like taking you out for a night on the town or giving back rubs every night or an especially thoughtful gift."

I knew a man who thought he was demonstrating his love for his wife by making improvements to their home. But she saw his behavior as self-indulgent rather than loving, and she wanted something different: more communication and connection. They fell into an escalating struggle in which she asked for affection, which he thought he was demonstrating with his handiwork. The more he tried to demonstrate his love, the less love she felt. Luckily, before it was too late, they realized that they had different ways of establishing an emotional connection.

That men and women use different means to attract each other seems obvious, and research backs this up. For example, men tend to use displays of their resources and wealth to attract women, whereas women rely more on making themselves physically attractive (Campbell and Ellis 2005). Anyone who has been to a singles bar could tell you that, and most of us don't judge either strategy to be wrong; they're just different.

But as relationships mature, we tend to view the male way of expressing love as incorrect. My profession doesn't help. Psychology is a word-based endeavor. We repair relationships mostly by talking about them, and we tend to impose that on men.

I'm not suggesting that men can't improve their communication. But there is value in recognizing that the male way of connecting is an attempt to create intimacy, even if it's different from the ways of connecting that most women prefer.

Men tend to express love actively. He may not talk about it much, but a man who changes your oil might as well be reading you love poems. We simply find clean oil to be more useful than Lord Byron's "She Walks in Beauty" because we want you to be safe and happy.

How Men Think

"It seems like I can knock myself out doing repairs, cutting firewood, working on the cars, and even doing housework, but somehow there's an issue with what I *haven't* done. That really makes me retreat."

For the Man in Your Life:
A Simple Task

In the survey that I conducted while writing this book, a lot of guys complained that they take flack from women for trying to fix their problems. There were comments like "Why does she complain about her boss, her family, or the rattle in her dashboard and then get mad when I offer a solution?"

When a woman complains but declines our solutions (or worse, gets angry at us) it feels like she's saying, *Here's a way that you can make me happy, but I just want you to listen to it. I don't want you to actually do it.* It's like taking a dog to a park, showing him the tennis ball he loves to chase, and then putting that ball back in your pocket.

We men contribute to the pattern when we become frustrated and argue that women should listen to our solutions. There's a better way. If you're a task-driven man—if you demonstrate your love by doing rather than talking—try reframing things a bit. When the woman in your life begins to discuss a problem with you, ask her what she wants from you. Does she want to explore ways to fix it, or does she simply want to discuss it for now?

If she simply wants to converse, which is a perfectly reasonable thing to ask, then conversing is your job. The task is to pay attention, understand what she's saying, and participate in the conversation. Do it correctly, and do it as effectively as you would do any other task. There's no need to make it more complicated than that.

Chapter 3

The Expectation Shift

Let's take brief inventory of the first two chapters. Men want to mate for the long term. We demonstrate our love by being useful. We want to be the most important thing to the women in our lives. We're vulnerable to pain, but acknowledging our vulnerability violates the rule of stoicism. Oh, and we couldn't care less about the kind of car a woman drives.

These male qualities create unique challenges when we finally earn a woman's love and relationship expectations begin to develop. Sometimes expectations shift over the course of the relationship; sometimes they remain constant. Either way, men often find themselves wondering just what the heck they're supposed to do to keep earning a woman's love.

Researchers who look back at the way men and women have related over the millennia rarely wrote about love until recently. Instead, they've used rather sterile terms like "pair bonding," which refers to men and women maintaining long-term commitments to each other, usually in the service of raising children.

Pair bonding would seem to require a special ingredient in order to succeed. Maybe we could call it "love." As it turns out, pair bonding transcends time and culture. People have been doing it for a long, long time, but not always exclusively.

Humans have a long history with arrangements like polygyny (one man with two or more concurrent wives), serial monogamy, secret affairs, cuckoldry, and sometimes even polyandry (one woman with two or more concurrent husbands).

It might seem as though humans—mainly men—have been ambivalent about monogamy from the beginning. The majority of cultures have endorsed some form of polygyny (Murdoch 1967). Perhaps this can be boiled down to the fact that humans *really* like sex. But that doesn't mean that monogamy is necessarily a burden for men. After all, we routinely choose to engage in it. Rock stars and politicians aside, the males of our species seem to value monogamy—for the sake of the kids, if nothing else.

For men, sex is only part of the picture, which brings us back to that sterile old term, "pair bonding." From a pragmatic standpoint, pair bonding is the most successful strategy for a man and woman to ensure the survival of their offspring. That may be why, even though men and women alike have historically enjoyed sampling different lovers, pair bonding—and the love that comes with it—transcends time and culture (Campbell and Ellis 2005).

So if we're meant to bond in pairs, why do men and women drive each other so flippin' crazy sometimes? I think part of the reason lies in two trends that I see in my practice on a regular basis: the qualities that women are drawn to during courtship aren't necessarily the qualities they want in a long-term mate, and the male qualities that are most attractive during courtship can become irritating or offensive when the flip sides of those qualities eventually reveal themselves.

Men and women both change as a relationship matures, but men seem especially prone to the kind of change that leaves women wondering what happened to the person they fell in love with.

From Bad Boy to Altar Boy

Imagine a pair of prehistoric parents on the savanna. They would have had the same basic concerns as today's parents: feeding the children, keeping a roof over their heads, keeping the minivan gassed up. Well, maybe gasoline wasn't an issue, but they would have worried about other resources.

Because the world was simpler and harsher back then, it's tempting to think of our ancestors as simplified version of ourselves. That's not quite true. Our ancestors were probably every bit as complex as we are, but the harshness of the environment would have brought their survival-driven traits to the surface.

Choosing a suitable mate is one of the things that affects survival, and it certainly affects the survival of offspring. Both men and women would have wanted to pick out the best possible teammate with whom to face the world and rear their children. However, that doesn't mean prehistoric eyes didn't wander. If they were like us, mating was a complex mix of monogamy and polygamy for both men and women.

Sex and the Single Prehistoric Girl

One of the most confusing challenges for the modern man is decoding women's desires. Do women want the bad boy who's adventurous and exciting? Do they want an altar boy who's good, reliable, and slightly boring? Do they want a mix of the two? Prehistoric men may have been just as confused as we are today because, as it turns out, women's desires are complex, and they can shift when we befuddled men least expect it.

For example, researchers have found that women's sexual fantasies frequently include having sex with more than one man, and those fantasies are most common when women are in the fertile phase of their cycle. In fact, that's when modern women are most likely to engage in affairs outside their relationship or have sex with multiple partners within a brief period of time, which may promote sperm competition (Nummi and Pellikka 2012). (Sperm competition, in turn, results in stronger offspring because the sperm of healthier and more potent men tend to reach the egg before the sperm of less healthy and potent men when both are, shall we say, swimming in the same race at the same time.)

How might that have played out on the savanna long ago? Whenever a woman got pregnant, she surely would have wanted the father around for protection. Pregnancy and the baby's early childhood were vulnerable times. But her motives for getting pregnant were quite complex, and they weren't limited to fantasies of a Paleolithic Prince Charming devoting his everlasting love to her. She was no fool, nor was she particularly chaste.

When a prehistoric woman was interested in short-term mating, as she would have been during the fertile period of her cycle, she might have preferred men with overt signs of testosterone, such as a muscular build and a masculine face (Schmitt 2005). These guys would also have had a strong sex drive, low commitment, and high promiscuity—great sperm, but not the best hubby material.

For a good, long-term mate, she probably would have preferred a man with stability, devotion, and a good ability to provide for the kids. In other words, she might want to mate with prehistoric Fonzie, but she would want to pair with a nice, boring, Richie Cunningham type.

The stereotype of a prehistoric woman at the whim of club-wielding men who made all the decisions about mating is a cartoonish departure from what's likely to have been the case. Far from being helpless, she would have exerted a lot of control over who got her pregnant and who raised her children—and they may not have been the same man.

What about the men of the times? What would they have wanted? The old idea that prehistoric men wanted sex with as many women as possible is also an oversimplification. Like modern men, they would have experienced the urge to pair up with a special lady, and they would have tried to keep her around.

According to recent research, a prehistoric man's methods for keeping a woman's attention would have varied with his status. If he were a low-value mate (meaning he had low social status, was unattractive, or had some other shortcoming), he would have been likely to compel her to stay by hurting her, insulting her to lower her self-esteem, or otherwise applying unpleasant pressure to limit her freedom. If he were a high-value mate

How Men Think

"I think women have a hard time understanding what kind of guy is good for them. They often choose men who others can clearly see are bad for them, then complain about the results. They like confident men. Well, men are rarely superconfident around women they care about. They are, however, confident around women they don't care about. This attracts women to men who don't like them much. Guys can see this a million miles away. Women seem blind to it."

(good-looking, socially connected, and wealthy), he would have tried to earn her continuing affection by providing benefits like resources and romance—the very things the low-status man would have difficulty providing (Starratt and Shackelford 2012).

That's not so different from the way things work today. High-value men still tend to treat women better (Starratt and Shackelford 2012). They try to keep a woman invested in the relationship by complimenting her, giving her gifts, and generally trying to maintain her affection, rather than being possessive.

But I'm digressing a bit too far. The point is that prehistoric men had ways of trying to maintain monogamy, even if they had the same urges for promiscuity that modern men possess, while women exerted a great deal of control over whose child they carried. Our distant ancestors' love lives were more complex than we've been led to believe.

Fast-Forward a Few Millennia

The same romantic circuitry that existed in prehistoric lovers resides in us today. Men still have more of a penchant for promiscuity than women, but most men tend toward monogamy. One study asked people how many different sex partners they would ideally like to have in the next month. In North America, 23 percent of men but only 3 percent of women said they would like to have more than one partner (Schmitt et al. 2003). The figures for males across ten regions globally ranged from a low of 17.9 percent in East Asia to a high of 35 percent in South America, whereas those for women ranged from 2.6 in East Asia to 7.1 percent in Eastern Europe, indicating that the desire for some degree of promiscuity is generally higher in men.

That doesn't mean men typically do what they want, it just means they have these urges. Women have these urges too. In one study of Western women, one in four women acknowledged infidelity, one in eight admitted to having sex with two or more males in a twenty-four-hour period, and one in twelve said they'd had sexual threesomes with two men (Gallup, Burch, and Berens Mitchell 2006).

More importantly—and this is where it gets confusing for men—a body of research indicates that women's preferences in men can change with their menstrual cycle. Women in the fertile phase of their cycle are especially attracted to more masculine faces, bodies, voices, and scents, and there's some evidence that they are more highly attracted to intelligence. On average, women report stronger attraction to men other than their partners during this phase, especially when their partners are relatively lacking in these features (Gangestad and Thornhill 2003; Gangestad, Thornhill, and Garver-Apgar 2010).

When women aren't in the fertile phase, their tastes tend to revert back to the more stable and less aggressive or exciting kind of man—the kind of guy who is more likely to invest exclusively in one mate. A guy like that typically has physical features that correspond with lower testosterone.

I don't want to overstate the matter. It's not as if women prefer Rocky Balboa on Tuesday and Mr. Mom on Friday. The effects are subtle, which is why men and women probably don't notice them on a day-to-day basis. Plus, it's possible that some people are essentially unaffected by these ancient drives.

Nevertheless, the complexity of women's desires is enough to leave men wondering who they should be and how they should behave. Do women want the bad boy, or do they want the altar boy? It seems that through the ages, women have wanted both, but not necessarily at the same time.

Being ever motivated to earn your affection, it seems that we men are wired to give you both. It appears that we're equipped to be the bad boy when we're trying to win you over, and the altar boy after we win your love. Another way to put it is that we seem to show off our more masculine, Fonzie-like traits when we're trying to earn your love, but we switch to reliable Richie Cunningham mode once we have a relationship (and possibly offspring) to protect.

This arrangement can be as frustrating for women as it is for men. One woman put it this way: "Men who are strong and ambitious are frequently arrogant and sexist. They certainly don't want to deal with the emotional terrain of a relationship. Nice guys complain that they never get ahead, but they rarely ask for what they want. Sensitivity and guts seem to be mutually exclusive."

Men seem equipped to adapt to women's varying expectations, but with varying degrees of success, as evidenced by the complaint in the above quotation. While adapting to a woman's desires sounds like an efficient mating strategy in theory, it's difficult to strike the perfect balance. Sometimes men don't change enough, and sometimes they change too much.

Believe It or Not, Men Worry About the Relationship Too

Because men are so stoic, it's easy to forget that we worry about the relationship too. Perhaps that's also because some of our worries are counterintuitive to women.

For example, many men worry that the woman in their lives will find them unattractive if they show vulnerability, whereas she may feel that vulnerability builds intimacy. Or a man may worry that if he admits a mistake, his partner will throw it back in his face, which will drive them apart. She, on the other hand, may feel that his honesty brings them closer.

Here's another common issue: Many men fear that they won't be able to keep up or defend themselves if a woman starts discussing complaints from the past. Therefore, they tend to shut down at the first sign of old arguments. Women, on the other hand, might view conversations about the past as ones that bring them closer to the men in their lives.

Plato is reputed to have said, "Be kind, for everyone you meet is fighting a hard battle." Even the guy who carries himself like James Dean has more than a few preoccupations and relationship worries. As one man put it, "I wish I could read women's minds." Translation: We worry about what you're thinking too.

"He Wasn't That Way When I Met Him"

Enough scientific preamble. Let's get down to practicalities. A lot of women complain that the man they fell in love with used to be exciting but is now boring. What happened to that talkative, resourceful, adventurous man? Here's how one woman put it: "Why do men get comfortable and stop trying to impress their women? All the things she fell in love with in the beginning come to an end, making her wonder if it was all an act."

I myself am an example. My wife has pointed out that since we married I've become hesitant to do many of the playful things I did when we were dating, like riding bikes and taking day trips to the mountains. Somewhere along the line, I became all business. I grew up, or I became boring—it depends on how you frame it. I'm not even sure when it happened.

Men tend to ride into relationships like heroes only to discover that our courting persona is a tough act to follow. We start out with princely charm and roguish charisma. Then somehow we end up with a spare tire and sparingly few words. Women can end up feeling disappointed, while we end up wondering what went wrong.

Expectation Shift 1: "He's Not the Man I Married"

As relationships mature and change, one of the challenges men face involves some of the same relationship dynamics that existed long ago, with early humans: the qualities that women are drawn to during court-ship aren't necessarily the qualities they want in a long-term mate. Young men often feel that they have to put on airs to attract women, and older men often feel that they must behave as if they've been domesticated.

Here's how one man in his twenties described his frustration with courtship:

> "When I'm talking to women, I feel like I have to pretend to be edgy or aggressive. That's not really me, but if I don't put on that mask, women lose interest."

Now, here's a married man in his thirties, well after the courtship has ended:

> "Men are so basic, so easy to keep happy. I think this frustrates women in a way. I think many women want us to meet them on the more emotional plane, but that contradicts what attracted them to us in the beginning. They want the strong, silent type or the bad boy, but once the relationship is up and running they want us to be more sensitive and open to talking about more things. Unfortunately, I don't think you can have it both ways."

Finally, here are the tired sentiments of a married man in his fifties:

> "I often hear jokes about how the best marriages are the ones where the man passively says, 'Yes, dear.' Sure, I suppose that avoids conflict and gives women all the control that some might desire, but it seems to remove the inner drive and spirit that might have originally attracted a woman in the first place."

Each of these men, in the respective stages of their relationships, seems confused and concerned about their effectiveness. Each of them seems to be wondering, *How the heck am I supposed to behave?*

I've spoken to many recently married young men who understand that their partner's expectations have shifted, but often they're unable to verbalize what is now expected of them. At the same time, their own behavior is changing, and they notice that they're no longer as adventurous or attentive as they once were.

Sometimes that's due to the male tendency to stop working so hard once we've earned a woman's love. Sometimes it's due to the friction that arises from women's expectation that we change (often that we give up our adventurous ways) and our failure to do so.

In either case, communication and being clear about expectations can prevent a world of heartache. When both men and women understand their shifting expectations, they're much better able to negotiate their roles as the relationship matures.

Expectation Shift 2: "It Used to Be Cute When He Did That"

Sometimes the shift in relationship expectations has less to do with ancient drives than the simple fact that our good qualities—the qualities that attract our mates—can have an annoying side. In other words, it can become a problem when a man *doesn't* change as the relationship evolves.

I met Tyrone and Samantha after they'd been married for about two years. Samantha felt that Tyrone had become overbearing, opinionated, and bossy. She said that the problem had started about six months into their marriage.

When I asked Samantha what first drew her to Tyrone, she said she'd loved his charisma, his decisiveness, and the fact that he was a natural-born leader.

From my safe distance, I could easily see that being opinionated and being decisive are two sides of the same coin. The same is true with bossiness and leadership, as well as being overbearing and having charisma. But Samantha, who was in the common position of failing to see the forest for the trees, didn't recognize that the very qualities that first drew her to Tyrone—some of his strongest traits—were the same qualities that came to annoy her and even leave her feeling a bit oppressed.

In the beginning of the relationship, she loved his take-charge attitude. She loved that he organized their dates, that he always drove, that he paid the bill at restaurants, and that he held the door for her. But as time wore on, she realized that Tyrone's assertiveness interfered with her ability to express her own desires. She still admired his strong character, but she didn't want him to be too assertive, nor did she want him to be a wimp. Like Goldilocks, she wanted his level of assertiveness to be just right.

Tyrone was experiencing a complementary problem as their relationship matured. One of the qualities that drew him to Samantha was her good-natured patience. About six months into the marriage, he began to wonder why she was becoming so argumentative and unhappy. Like any good man, he wanted his partner to be satisfied and joyful. He didn't realize that his strongest qualities were becoming an irritant.

This type of expectation shift isn't unique to women. It works both ways. The man who marries a woman for her intelligence can become frustrated when she intellectualizes their arguments, and the woman who marries a man whose industriousness she admires can become lonely when he misses dinner in order to put in a few more hours at the office. However, in my clinical experience, this problem is especially confusing and frustrating for men precisely because they so often feel a sense of duty and a desire to be effective. A shift in expectations, such as Samantha's wish that Tyrone would stop being so strong-willed with her, can leave a duty-bound man feeling as if he's failing at the relationship.

What Men Struggle With

Men loathe the feeling of failing at the relationship. We live for women, and we're out of sorts when we don't know how to be useful to you. Let's quickly review the problems men experience when trying to win women's affection:

* We can sense when we aren't pleasing you, but we don't often know what to do about it.

* We are deeply affected by your mood. When you're unhappy, we're unhappy.

* The rule of stoicism prevents us from approaching you when we're worried, hurt, or frustrated.

* We sometimes lack the training or willingness to put words to our thoughts or emotions.

* We often assume that relationship problems are our fault because we're taught that the female way of relating is the correct way.

* We tend to put our emotions behind secondary expressions like anger, humor, or withdrawal.

* We're thrown off-kilter when expectations shift in the relationship.

Don't get me wrong. I'm not whining on behalf of men. We are men after all, and what do men do? We fix things! Or at least we try.

In part 2 of the book, I'm going to show you what it looks like when a man is trying to solve a relationship problem. It can be easy to miss because male problem-solving strategies are often different from women's, and they don't always work out.

Still, male problem-solving strategies are reasonable from a certain point of view, and sometimes they actually work.

For the Man in Your Life:
Handling the Expectation Shift

You've probably heard women complain about the men in their lives going through a sad metamorphosis.

- "He used to be fun."

- "What happened to the romance?"

- "He's just not the adventurous guy he used to be."

You've probably also heard men complain about changes in their wives and girlfriends.

- "She used to be fun."

- "She never used to nag me."

- "When did she turn into her mother?"

Women tend to complain that men get boring with age; men tend to complain that women become more demanding. Expectations change as a relationship matures, and we men sometimes have trouble adjusting.

It's hard enough for us to talk about the relationship when things are going well, and some of us really clam up when it's time to discuss changes. But retreating from those conversations can cost us our integrity, and it can make the women in our lives truly unhappy.

I knew a guy who had a high sense of what it meant to be a man. He believed that a man should be industrious and honorable, and that he should spare nothing to serve his family.

This strong man married an equally strong woman who was equally opinionated. Their values and their personalities seemed perfectly aligned. But as the relationship matured, their strength and candor turned into bickering. They began to have power struggles, and he found it easier to back away from arguments than to disagree with his wife. *Maybe she'll be happy if I stop arguing*, he thought. *At least I won't be making things worse.*

But it did make things worse. His withdrawal left her feeling insecure about the relationship, so she started pressing him to talk. The more she pressed, the more he withdrew into his garage, his golf game, and his bag of pot. He felt emasculated, and she felt lonely and disappointed. *He just isn't the same guy he used to be*, she thought. *He's a lump.*

When they finally realized what was happening—that he was withdrawing in order to keep peace—they made room in the relationship for the qualities she had fallen in love with.

He stopped backing away from her, she eased her approach to him, and they learned how to negotiate their differences. They were both happy again. (Incidentally, he stopped craving pot once he felt he had regained his masculinity.)

No matter what you bring into the relationship, be it a bundle of strong opinions or a penchant for soft music and candlelight, you have a responsibility to participate in forthright discussions about your partner's expectations of you.

Relationships change and grow. If a man doesn't change and grow with them, he's bound to lose his integrity by disappearing into the woodwork or responding in ways that don't fit with his values, like losing himself in a bag of pot or a bottle of vodka.

Life is short. Don't spend your precious days whining or retreating if your partner has become unhappy with you. Find a way to incorporate your qualities into the relationship.

That may mean having some actual conversations with your partner. Cut yourself some slack if you don't know where to start—you wouldn't be the first guy with that problem.

You might begin by bouncing your ideas off a trusted friend, or you can take a typically more efficient route and hire a professional to guide you through your changing relationship. There's no shame in paying for good advice that can help prevent a lifetime of struggle.

Part 2

Why Men Just Don't Make Sense Sometimes

There's a bias among psychologists, the media, and, well, seemingly most people: when it comes to relationships, women know best. There may be some truth to that—it may be why men tend to rely on women in matters of the heart. But men also possess relationship wisdom.

It's true that the male way of approaching relationship problems sometimes makes things worse, and some men just don't know when to stop digging themselves into a hole. But sometimes the male way of solving problems is quite effective, and sometimes the male way is actually the most useful way.

The wise couple doesn't discount the male relationship repertoire, even if it may seem unrefined. After all, as any good man will tell you, you can never have too many tools.

Chapter 4

The Male Way Is Sometimes the Most Useful Way

There's an old riddle about a farmer who returns from market, where he purchased a dog, a goose, and a head of cabbage. He has a small boat in which he can only transport himself and one item across a river to get home. If he leaves the dog alone with the goose, the dog will eat the goose. If he leaves the goose alone with the cabbage, the goose will eat the cabbage.

How does he get all three items safely across the river while making as few trips as possible? Go ahead and solve the riddle. I'll wait here.

Ready? Here's the answer: First, he takes the goose across the river and then goes back to the other side. Next, he takes the dog across and returns with the goose. He leaves the goose on the first side and takes the cabbage across. Now the dog and the cabbage are safely across the river. Finally, he returns for the goose. At no time did the dog have the opportunity to eat the goose, nor did the goose have the opportunity to eat the cabbage.

What does any of this have to do with harmony between the genders? Quite a bit. It illustrates the fact that different kinds of problems require different problem-solving strategies. You may have noticed that men and women tend to approach things differently, to put it mildly.

If you tried to solve the river riddle, how did you go about it? Did you take a collaborative approach, gathering a group of friends to brainstorm solutions? Or did you take a more individualistic approach, like sketching the solution on a piece of paper or visualizing the farmer's journey in your mind?

Either approach would work, but an individualistic approach is more efficient for this kind of problem. In the time it would take you to gather your friends for a brainstorming session, you probably could have figured out the solution on your own.

Collaborative approaches are sometimes most appropriate, but they aren't all they're cracked up to be. Brainstorming—that collaborative problem-solving process in which a group generates as many ideas as possible while withholding criticism—dates back to the 1940s when an advertising executive named Alex Osborn wrote a book called *Your Creative Power* (1948). He devoted an entire chapter to this collaborative problem-solving approach. At first glance, it seems to make perfect sense: the more people "storming" a problem like commandos, the more answers they'll generate, right?

Wrong, as it turns out. Brainstorming was unceremoniously discredited in 1958 (and has been many times since), shortly after it had taken the business world by surprise. (You thought I was going to say "storm," didn't you?) A study out of Yale's psychology department found that people who participated in brainstorming sessions actually produced fewer creative solutions, and solutions of poorer quality, than those who worked individually (Taylor, Berry, and Block 1958).

That doesn't mean individual problem solving is always better. Sometimes collaboration is more effective, depending on the nature of the problem and the relationships between the collaborators. It helps if the participants are close enough that they can offer honest, critical feedback (Lehrer 2012).

The point is, sometimes collaboration works best, and sometimes the individual approach works best. The farmer's riddle is a good example of the latter—talking would just get in the way. Having written that statement, I can think of no more stereotypically male sentiment, or any more frequent source of irritation in relationships. Of course, we men don't mean to irritate, nor is it an accident that we approach problems the way we do.

Why Men Are Intrepid Problem Solvers

Have you ever wondered why men love Batman—why they want to *be* Batman? It's because Batman is resourceful. He has tools. He's the ultimate do-it-yourselfer. Batman is never caught with his pants (okay, tights) down, and he has the tenacity to solve any problem.

The real question is why men want to be able to solve any problem. Why not let somebody else handle it or wait until things work themselves out? And more to the point of this book, why do men feel the need to leap into action or offer solutions whenever women simply want to converse and connect?

The answer, unsurprisingly, is that resourcefulness makes us more attractive to women. (Have I mentioned yet how important you are to us?)

Human males aren't the only ones trying to impress the ladies. Male satin bowerbirds, found in Australia, are clever little guys who build impressive bird-sized gazebos made of grass and other materials that they gather from the surrounding area. They're named

> ## How Men Think
>
> **"Men are problem solvers. If you come to us with problems, our natural inclination is to try to fix them."**

61

after these bowers that they build. The purpose, as you've probably guessed, is to attract female bowerbirds, who shop around for the male with the most impressive bower.

Male bowerbirds are known to be rather intelligent, and a group of researchers wanted to learn to what degree the hens valued intelligence in their mates. To find out, they presented male bowerbirds with strange challenges to test their intelligence (Keagy, Savard, and Borgia 2009).

For example, the researchers anchored annoying colored tiles to the ground around the birds' carefully constructed bowers. The smart birds quickly learned that it was impossible for them to remove the tiles, so they camouflaged them. The researchers rank-ordered the male birds based on their performance, from most intelligent to least. Not surprisingly, the more intelligent males had greater mating success. That means either that intelligence helps the males attract hens, that hens prefer more intelligent males, or both. Either way, intelligence increases mating success.

It's hard to miss the similarity between the bowers these birds build and the houses, bridges, careers, and backyard decks that men build—all reasonable proxies of a man's intelligence. Of course, the size of a man's deck, or his brain, isn't readily apparent upon first meeting him, so we men have developed subtler ways of signaling our problem-solving ability.

Humor is one of our more important signals. It predicts intelligence, creativity, good genes, and good parenting traits. And guess what? Like a good bower, a good sense of humor predicts mating success—at least for men.

In general, men score higher on the ability to produce humor than woman, which suggests that the human sense of humor evolved, at least in part, as one indicator by which women can take the measure of a man (Greengross and Miller 2011). Maybe that's why men report that they try to be funnier when they flirt with women: it allows them to subtly transmit their underlying qualities (Wilbur and Campbell 2011).

And in fact, women don't merely appreciate humor, they subconsciously use it to evaluate men, taking it as a sign of intelligence and warmth (Wilbur and Campbell 2011). It also serves as a simple indication that a man might be interested in a woman. (In case you're wondering, men also value humor in women, but they evaluate it differently. A man won't typically rule out a woman because she isn't funny.)

Here's one last bit of evidence that humor, which is an indication of intelligence, is intertwined with romance: Both men and women rate humor as highly important in a prospective mate (though women measure it with a more evaluative eye). We think people are funnier when we're interested in them, and we attempt to be funnier when we're trying to draw their attention. Humor serves as an indication of interest, especially early in relationships (Li et al. 2009).

When I asked women what they like most about men, humor and intelligence were both at the top of the list. Here are some of their responses:

* "What I like most about men is their boyishness. The sense of humor and play that some men have is by far what's most attractive."

* "What do I like most? Their sense of humor, their masculinity, and strength."

* "Humor. Protectiveness. Strength."

Men want to be resourceful because it makes us more attractive—at least in theory. But men tend to err on the side of overkill, and we often try to be clever even when doing so works against us.

Many women who took my survey told me that the male problem-solving instinct becomes distinctly unattractive when we misread the situation and offer unwanted solutions. I'll return to that topic later. First, let's look at how men generally approach problems. Like Batman, men often retreat into caves, and that is no small source of friction between men and women.

Mangineering

How many men does it take to change a lightbulb? Every good man knows the answer: one. Changing a lightbulb is not a group activity. Unless a man is in a submarine or a coal mine, replacing a lightbulb is more of a nuisance than a problem, and he isn't likely to spend much time discussing it or thinking about it. And even for more complex problems, we lean toward a manly, stoic way of hammering out solutions. I like to call it "mangineering." This approach involves shutting our pie-holes, putting our hands on the problem, and eradicating it so we can move on to the next challenge.

I come from a long, proud line of mangineers. It's a great strategy for some things, and an awful strategy for others. In any case, I want you to know what male problem solving looks like because it sometimes creates the impression that we don't care, when in fact we're working quite hard on a problem within the confines of our minds. Mangineering has two distinct qualities: it's introspective, and it's mechanistic.

Male Problem Solving Is Introspective

Women tend to communicate early and often about a problem. Men are more likely to view communication as a tool, and when they see it as the wrong tool for the job, they believe it should be stored neatly in the toolbox. Many men seem to believe that the most important parts of solving a problem take place in their heads. That may be related to the different types of problems men and women excel in solving.

Women are better at what psychologists call divergent thinking tasks—for example, listing as many interesting and unusual uses for a brick as possible. That requires abilities such as thinking among many categories simultaneously and generating unusual responses.

Men tend to be better at insight tasks—open-ended, ill-defined problems. Here's an example: "If you have black socks and brown socks in a drawer, mixed in a ratio of four to five, how many socks will you have to remove to ensure a matching pair?" (Answer: Three. If your first two are black and brown, the third will match one of them.) That type of problem solving requires the ability to think deeply about a problem and generate novel, appropriate, goal-oriented solutions (Lin et al. 2012).

You may be thinking, *So what?* Well, divergent thinking tasks—the kind at which women excel—involve such skills as language, free association, and long-term memory. Divergent thinking tasks tend to be word based.

By contrast, the insight tasks at which men excel require different skills, such as the ability to visualize mechanical arrangements or imagine sequences of events. These tasks involve cognitive skills that are more nonverbal.

This is one of those areas in which it's tempting to overstate the differences between men and women. Each gender possesses both skill sets; neither gender has a monopoly on any of them. Some women are better at insight tasks than men, and some men are better at divergent thinking tasks than women. Nevertheless, most everyone is better at one than the other, and in general, men excel at insight tasks.

How Men Think

"Not talking means I'm thinking, especially if I'm in trouble with her. I'm thinking about how to make the situation better for both of us. I'm not clamming up or distancing myself."

To accompany these different skill sets, men and women tend to have different learning styles. In general, school-age boys do better than their female peers in individualistic, competitive learning environments. They become autonomous learners in endeavors like mathematics, and they don't mind working in solitude to solve complex problems. They tend to enjoy exercising their independence, and they aren't afraid to take risks and invent new solutions. Girls, on the other hand, tend to follow standard problem-solving procedures in disciplines such as math. They tend to be more risk averse and less inventive in this particular arena (Catsambis 2005).

None of that suggests that boys are superior to girls at math. In fact, there's evidence that the genders are generally equally skilled, though there are more men at the extreme high and low ends of the IQ scale (Deary et al. 2003). Instead, it seems that math problems, and the environments in which they appear, may be better suited to the individualistic problem-solving style of boys.

One group of researchers asked secondary-school students to solve physics problems in same-gender and mixed-gender pairs (Harskamp, Ding, and Suhre 2008). The same-gender pairs had similar outcomes, despite the distinctly different problem-solving approaches. For the girls in mixed-gender pairs, however, outcomes suffered slightly. They didn't learn as much as the boys in mixed-gender pairs, the girls in same-gender pairs, or the boys in same-gender pairs. If this experiment is any indication, male and female styles of problem solving are similarly effective, but they don't always mix well, even when dealing with straightforward problems.

The individualistic way in which many men approach problems includes behaviors and characteristics that, while often effective, can be off-putting to someone who prefers more of a team approach:

* Men rely on themselves to generate an understanding of the situation before seeking the assistance of others.

* They tend to act before consulting, rather than consulting before acting.

* For men, solutions matter more than process.

* When working together, men rely on nonverbal communication more than women. (If you'd like a demonstration of the difference, watch two men move a couch, then watch two women do the same thing.)

* Men often see problem solving as an opportunity to demonstrate effectiveness, rather than an opportunity to connect with others.

Let's take a brief but necessary aside to discuss that last bullet point. The introspective nature of male problem solving shouldn't be confused with being individualistic or antisocial. Men have gotten a bad rap for being overly autonomous and unsociable. That's because professionals, like myself, and books, like this one, tend to focus mainly on one kind of social interaction: one-on-one, intimate relationships—the kind of interaction in which women operate more effectively than men.

Men don't lack the skill or desire to connect with others. We're equally social, but in a different way. While women tend to excel in small groups with intimate relationships, men function better in large groups with looser relationships. Group endeavors ranging from hunting parties to accounting firms are routinely more attractive to men.

That doesn't mean women can't function well on teams any more than it means men can't function well in intimate relationships. It just means that men tend to be more interested in groups, and they function particularly well in those settings. This starts in childhood, when girls prefer to play in pairs, whereas boys prefer groups. And when tasked with a problem to solve, girls do better in pairs and boys do better in groups (Benenson and Heath 2006).

As discussed in chapter 1, men are driven to be productive members of successful groups. We are social creatures, like women. But we also like to work alone, and we want to rely on our own resourcefulness sometimes.

Most of us aren't lone wolves. More often than not, our introspective approach just means we want to impress you or enjoy a small feeling of conquest by fixing something. Personally, I think it's the secret desire of every man to find a solution to a problem on his own, and then take it to his team and be a hero.

Men Need Teams

Women are generally more comfortable than men in closely connected relationships. Historically, women have focused their social efforts on small, intimate units more characterized by cooperation than competition.

Men, on the other hand, have historically been drawn to larger, loosely connected networks. Women can function in those networks too, every bit as effectively as men. The distinction just reflects how men and women have aligned themselves across cultures. Men like to join teams and compete with other men.

This difference in social preference matters a great deal in intimate relationships. Men can become overwhelmed by the level of intimacy at which women operate comfortably. We desire that intimacy, but we also want to be a cog in a larger system. This divides our attention and sometimes leaves women wondering how committed we are to an intimate relationship.

Most men need to be able to move between their intimate relationships and their teams. It doesn't mean we love you any less. In fact, just as we can feel pulled toward the team when we're with our partners, we're pulled toward our partners when we're working with the team. Ask any male soldier on deployment or any good man sent by his company to work overseas. In the midst of intense team activity, we are often most strongly drawn toward home and the people we love.

The happiest and most well-adjusted men have found a comfortable balance between love and teamwork. When a good man's loved ones are willing to let him go once in a while, he usually comes running back when he can.

Male Problem Solving Is Mechanistic

The second characteristic of mangineering is its mechanistic nature. Let's stay with the topic of math for a moment. Women tend to be underrepresented in math-intensive careers. It's tempting to blame that on some sort of male conspiracy or aptitude difference, but the simplest and most accurate explanation seems to be the one that's least discussed: men simply like numbers more than women. Women are equally capable, but not equally interested (Ceci and Williams 2010). A love of numbers seems to be a part of men's mechanistic view of things.

In his ironically titled book *Is There Anything Good About Men?* (he thinks there is), psychologist Roy Baumeister (2010) points out that men's entertainment is riddled with numbers, whereas women's entertainment isn't. Men's magazines, for example, are brimming with statistics related to sports, cars, guns, exercise, and anything else that interests men. He noted that even video games designed for boys and men involve statistics and numbers, such as numerical representations of strength. For men, numbers are fun. Baumeister also points out that numbers in women's entertainment are usually associated with something bad, like calories, but that, by and large, numbers just don't come up.

This affinity for numbers is just one example of how men are more mechanistic in their view of the world. I won't spend a lot of time making this case because, as professors like to say, some things are intuitively obvious. Torque wrenches and air compressors aren't marketed to women.

The mechanistic male approach to problem solving has some important implications that, again, can be quite effective but sometimes off-putting:

* Men see the world through a different lens than women.

* Men who rely on a mechanistic approach that has served them well may be at a loss when that approach is ill suited to nonmechanistic problems, like interpersonal difficulties.

* Men are comfortable with problems that involve an active and aggressive approach. Changing a tire comes to mind. That tire won't change itself. (Plus, solving a difficult problem like changing a tire without a jack is good for a few extra points on the man-card.)

* Men may approach nonmechanical problems, like interpersonal difficulties, with a mechanistic approach. For example, they may point out where their partner is failing, and do so at precisely the time that it's the least useful thing to discuss.

Why Men Crave Compliments

Does it seem like the man in your life needs to be stroked and complimented for every little thing? Does it feel like he's expecting a parade of gratitude every time he changes a lightbulb? If so, there's a good chance that he's trying to demonstrate his love with small acts of service. He may seek your gratitude as an indication that you love him too.

Unfortunately, supplying all of that gratitude can become a chore. If so, talk to him about it. Reassure him that you understand his intent. At the same time, keep in mind that each little active service is like saying, "I love you." Expressing gratitude may be less grating if you reframe it for yourself as a different way of saying, "I love you too."

The Law of Trying Harder

One of the things men are taught throughout their lives is to keep trying. We're taught that when a solution to a problem doesn't work, it's because we haven't put forth sufficient effort. If a boy has difficulty finding an answer to a problem like the riddle about the farmer crossing the river, the male figures in his life are likely to give him a scant clue and send him back to the drawing board with the directive to try harder. That teaches us perseverance, which is a useful and wonderful quality in many situations. In relationships, however, it can get in the way (something I'll take a closer look at in the next chapter).

Male problem solving is perfectly suited to problems like that riddle. To find the answer, a guy just needs to grind through the problem in a methodical, introspective, individualistic way. Mangineering means putting our boots in the stirrups, hands on the problem, or pen on paper. It means taking charge, being resourceful, and obliterating the problem so we can get on with life. It may not always be pretty, but it gets the job done. For the mangineer, the answer matters more than the process.

Still, sometimes it backfires. Men may be great at building and fixing things, but just as a person can become overly reliant on communication to fix any problem, the mangineer can become overly reliant on his individualistic and mechanistic approach.

Why Mangineering Is So Great...and So Challenging to Live With

Mangineering is great when results count, but results are only one consideration in relationships, where it's also important to consider things like companionship, connection, and collaboration. As useful as it can be, the male approach to problem solving can be challenging for women to live with. As one woman put it, "Their desire to solve problems overshadows women's attempts to communicate, even when men know that communication is what women want or need."

One of the reasons men get frustrated with the women in their lives involves orientation to time. The mangineering approach typically entails focusing on what's happening in the here and now. Men want to handle one problem at a time and move on. Many men have complained to me that their wives' or girlfriends' minds frequently operate in the past and future instead of the here and now. This can leave men feeling ill equipped for the conversation.

This difference in orientation can also be difficult for women, sometimes causing them to feel as if the men in their lives don't care about them, when in fact their men are trying to demonstrate their love. The situation that developed between a woman named Sandy and her husband, Justin, was an example of this. She would ask Justin to do small tasks, and he usually responded quickly. Whether it was attending to the baby, fixing the car, or anything else she asked, he leapt into action like Batman.

But Sandy felt as if Justin didn't understand what she needed from him. When she asked him to do something for the baby, for example, she thought back to the past and all of the times she had to ask him to do the same task. He wasn't noticing the pattern and anticipating her needs. She wondered why she had to keep asking him for the same things repeatedly and wondered if she'd have to nag him like this for the rest of their lives. She began to feel resentful that he never took initiative. She assumed that people who care about each other anticipate each other's needs. That's how she operated, so Justin's different approach seemed a bit distant and uncaring to her.

From Justin's point of view, he was demonstrating his love for her each time he fulfilled a request. Each new task was an opportunity to show his devotion. He was operating introspectively, mechanistically, and in the here and now. He didn't think ahead because he relied on his resourcefulness to help him solve any problem that came along—just like Batman. Meanwhile, he couldn't understand why Sandy was becoming so testy.

Luckily, these two caught the problem before the pattern took over their relationship. By bringing their different approaches out into the light, Sandy gained a new appreciation for Justin and his way of operating in the world, and Justin learned how much it would mean to Sandy if he thought ahead more often. They had to work at it, but they eventually got their time frames more in sync.

If you have a river to cross with your dog, your goose, and your cabbage, then male problem solving is the way to go. But the same qualities that make mangineering so useful in some contexts can be a burden in others. A man's individualistic thinking can leave his partner

How Men Think

"We care; we just show it differently. Our efficiency and economy of speech and action mean that, unless there's a problem to be fixed, we'll be happy just being with you."

feeling abandoned, and his mechanistic thinking can blind him to larger patterns.

For both women and men, simply becoming aware of differences in problem-solving strategies and how intentions are expressed can make relationships more satisfying and enjoyable.

For the Man in Your Life:
What Would the Marlboro Man Do?

Did you ever wonder what the Marlboro Man would do if the woman in his life was unhappy with him? Even he has a domestic life to tend to. He can't hide out on that horse all day.

Obviously, men and women approach relationship problems differently. Men tend to be hands-on fixers, with a focus on the here and now: *Let's focus on the problem in front of us and fix it fast.*

Women tend to focus on larger patterns and devote more attention to the past and future: *Let's talk about the times this has happened before so we can prevent it from happening again.*

I think these differences are one of the main reasons that communication can break down between men and women. But regardless of the particular communication problems in any given relationship, this much is true: men are more likely than women to walk away from a conversation when the going gets tough, and that only makes things worse.

Sure, sometimes women give us the silent treatment. But let's not split hairs. Guys have a greater tendency to retreat rather than endure what seems like miserable, endless discourse on the state of the relationship. Sometimes we retreat into productive things like work. Sometimes we retreat into nothing more impressive than a video game or a six-pack. Whatever that retreat looks like on the surface, it leaves women feeling abandoned and even more motivated to force us into that dreaded conversation.

Men often try to look tough and stoic when retreating from women. A typical thought is *A man doesn't sit around all day and talk.* I should know. I come from a long line of retreaters, and I struggle with it to this day. But I've come to realize that retreating from a problem with the woman I love is far from the manliest thing to do.

Take a look at guys who refuse to face up to relationship problems. How many of them have substance-abuse problems, poor health, broken relationships, and kids they only see with a judge's permission? Their stoicism clearly isn't working out very well.

Sure, stoicism is one of the more important masculine traits. But it exists so we can help ourselves and others to survive difficult times, not to serve as a barrier that prevents us from solving problems. The most masculine men I know have solid relationships because they're willing to discuss problems, before those problems get out of hand. They also know how to obtain assistance from their family, friends, the church, the dojo, and even therapists. Assistance is all around us, and it seems to magically appear when we become willing to use it.

Look at it this way: You wouldn't drive around with a flat tire, hands over your ears, shouting, "La, la, la, the car is fine!" Why let a relationship fall into disrepair? The Marlboro Man might be intimidated by talking, but I'll bet he doesn't let that fear stand in his way.

Chapter 5

The Male Way Is Sometimes the Least Useful Way

O scar and Maria had enjoyed a mostly happy and untroubled marriage for nearly twenty years. Like any married couple, they had their points of friction, often revolving around Maria's complaint that Oscar too often took matters into his own hands. Oscar, on the other hand, sometimes felt that Maria didn't appreciate the little things he did for her.

They sometimes joked that problems were like little gifts from heaven for Oscar. He couldn't wait to get his hands on anything that needed to be fixed, even if Maria didn't really want his solution. For example, she once commented that their spice rack was inadequate. Two weeks later, he presented her with a monstrosity of a spice rack—or so it seemed to her. It looked as if it were designed to hold every known spice and to withstand the most punishing spice experiences.

Maria was good-natured about the spice rack. She thanked Oscar, and he mounted it on the kitchen wall. But his solutions didn't always work so smoothly.

By the time their daughter, Christie, was about to turn sixteen, she was a skilled piano player. One day Oscar heard Maria and Christie discussing a new baby grand piano as a gift for her sixteenth birthday. Over the next few weeks, he noticed them looking through catalogs, scrolling through online reviews, and seeming to agonize over the decision.

You can probably guess what happened next. Oscar saw the opportunity to solve two problems at once. He could please his daughter and wife, and he could also spare them the apparently awful experience of shopping for the piano. To Oscar, it looked like his wife and daughter were lost in piano land, and he intended to rescue them.

Surreptitiously, he talked to a salesman, purchased the best baby grand piano the family could afford, and had it delivered when he knew his wife and daughter would be out. He expected them to be thrilled when they saw what he had done, but they seemed unenthusiastic. Although his daughter expressed gratitude, he could sense that she was unhappy.

Later that evening, in private, Maria scolded Oscar for purchasing the piano. Hurt and angry, Oscar said, "How can you be mad at me? I was just trying to do something nice for both of you!"

"We didn't need your help," Maria answered. Oscar felt crushed, and Maria was hurt. He didn't understand that they considered shopping for the piano to be a bonding experience, not a burden. Oscar saw the situation as an equation to be solved, and the lack of gratitude left him feeling baffled and hurt.

Why Men Dig the Hole Deeper and Deeper

You would think that a clever, industrious guy like Oscar would notice that his strategy wasn't working—that his attempts to fix things and bring happiness frequently had the opposite effect. It isn't solely a male trait to dig oneself deeper and deeper into a hole. As we humans find our way through life, we discover problem-solving strategies that work for us and become attached to them as old standbys we can turn to in a pinch. The more serious the problem, the more we rely on our old tried-and-true strategies. Unfortunately, we often fail to recognize when these old stand-bys are failing us.

This is one of the reasons why anxiety is such an insidious condition. The strategies people use to manage anxiety have worked well in other contexts, but they fail when applied to thoughts and feelings. For example, people may have learned that avoiding frightening things like snakes or spiders helps them avoid the unpleasant experience of fear. But when anxiety comes from inside, perhaps in the form of a painful memory or self-doubt, that old standby strategy of escape will only make things worse for basically the same reason that trying not to think of monkeys forces you to think about monkeys (Wegner et al. 1987). That's just the nature of anxiety. (I'll discuss this further in the next chapter because it's important to relationships.)

Yet even when our problem-solving strategies make a situation worse, we seem to have difficulty recognizing it because we feel an increasing urge to solve the now-more-difficult problem. Instead, we tend to try harder and harder using the same old strategies, and the more they fail us, the more likely we are to use them again and again out of desperation.

Somewhere in Oscar's history, he had learned that fixing problems for people made them happy, which in turn made him feel happy, useful, and effective. When that strategy failed in his relationship, he became more desperate to be effective and tightened his grip on his favorite tool: taking charge and fixing problems.

To make matters more complicated, sometimes his strategy did work within his relationship. Sometimes Maria genuinely appreciated his solutions. That helped keep him stuck in the pattern. As with a slot machine, winning once in a while compels a person to keep trying. An intermittent reward is a powerful motivator, and somewhere deep down, Oscar's mind probably figured he'd eventually succeed if he just kept trying harder. You can't blame Oscar for trying what had worked in the past, but he needs to figure out when to use what is simultaneously one of his most and least useful relationship skills.

Men like Oscar aren't inept—far from it. Clearly, they are resourceful and fiercely devoted to their loved ones. But they are often unskilled at putting words to their own internal experiences, and that makes it difficult to recognize when the hole is getting deeper.

Oscar, like many other men, knew there was a problem, and he was suffering because of it. He clearly prided himself on caring for his family. To hear that he was ineffective would strike him at his core. Let's look at what kept him from properly addressing the situation.

Men's Emotional Training

This section should really be titled "Men's Nonemotional Training" because we are seldom taught to exist peacefully with our emotions. Sure, we learn to handle emotions like fear and frustration, but we are given little instruction about others, such as sadness and anxiety. That sometimes leaves us ill prepared to handle relationship difficulties.

In a study of how depression is characterized in men's magazines such as *Sports Illustrated*, *Esquire*, and *Men's Health*, sociologist and professor of gender studies Juanne Clarke (2009) found that depression is typically presented to men as a biochemical or genetic problem—right in line with the mechanistic way in which men tend to view the world. Men are rarely taught to think of sadness or depression as a reasonable response to difficult situations, or as something that might be remedied by exploring the emotions themselves to discover where they come from.

In her study, Clarke found that men's magazines typically profiled highly successful men who had overcome the supposedly biological "disease" of depression. And by and large, their approach to defeating depression involved aggressive medication rather than treating root causes or making lifestyle changes.

Even physicians get drawn into this way of viewing depression. Feelings of sadness and despair that lead women to be diagnosed with depression are often overlooked by doctors when they appear in men. Men commit suicide three to four times more often than women, and they turn to alcohol and drugs at least twice as frequently as women because they, and the people around them, often fail to recognize their depression for what it is. One of the reasons depression is diagnosed twice as often among women is because men are less likely to notice and identify feelings of sadness.

How Men Think

"I'm not some emotionless caveman whose sole purpose is to get laid. I have a lot of emotional depth. It's just that I feel uncomfortable expressing my emotions unless I'm very close to someone. Otherwise, I do my best to stonewall any unpleasant emotions if possible."

While we're on the topic of depression, men sometimes express a unique cluster of symptoms when depressed. Because they're taught to suck it up and reject vulnerable emotions or bad moods, they tend to display symptoms that are more masculine on the surface but also more destructive. Whereas women tend to look for the source of their depression, men typically try to hammer their emotions into line by doing things like abusing alcohol or embracing anger. In fact, men who turn to more "masculine" expressions of sadness are more likely to be fearful of and avoid negative emotions (Green and Addis 2012).

One group of researchers found that fear of emotions prevents men from developing healthier responses to depression. In nearly every country in the world, more men than women die by suicide, often following a loss such as unemployment, a business failure, a broken relationship, or an embarrassing public disclosure (Coleman, Kaplan, and Casey 2011). When a man has an intolerably low view of himself and a restricted range of emotional options, he's more likely to turn to ways of dealing with emotions that are acceptable within the male world, like emotional avoidance or self-destruction.

Men's approach to depression is an extreme example of the way men tend to handle emotions in general. We're socialized not to discuss our emotions and even to avoid them within ourselves. If the research is correct, men avoid emotions that make them vulnerable, even if the costs are high. Oscar undoubtedly found disapproval from his wife and daughter terribly painful, but that might be the last thing that he'd admit, or perhaps even recognize. To do so would be to acknowledge his vulnerability. To the average male mind, vulnerability means weakness, and that's unacceptable.

How Men Think

"We don't feel the same way women feel, but we certainly feel. We might express things differently because of our biology and how we're socialized, but we're not all that different. We can all be weak, vulnerable to setbacks, prone to failure, and unsatisfied. And in the end, we all want to be loved and respected."

So, what do men do when they feel vulnerable? They turn to their old standbys. Some men avoid or escape what seems like an intolerable situation through video games, alcohol, golf—anything that draws attention away from painful thoughts and feelings. Other men invoke the law of trying harder, as Oscar did. He wasn't trying to create problems when he bought the piano. He was trying to fix a problem and get closer to the women in his life. But his lack of emotional training blinded him to the true nature of the situation, and trying harder only served to alienate those he loved most.

It Takes Two

The old saying "It takes two to tango" is just as true in reverse, though less poetic: it takes two to create an ill-functioning relationship pattern. Whatever faults a man may bring into a relationship, he can't create relationship difficulties by himself.

It's tempting to blame Oscar for his problems with Maria. After all, it seems he should have recognized that his long history of jumping to solve problems sometimes made things worse. But we could also blame Maria for giving mixed signals. Sometimes she appreciated Oscar's efforts, and sometimes she found them hurtful; and through it all, she failed to adequately communicate what she really wanted from him.

Personally, I find it much more useful to focus on patterns that people create in relationships, rather than assigning blame. I'll discuss this approach in detail in chapter 7. For now, let's look at one of the most common patterns that women complain about: a man who shuts down whenever she tries to connect with him.

You might be wondering how I could possibly suggest that a woman has anything to do with a man shutting down and failing to communicate, especially after I've made the case that men tend toward stoicism, that we have difficulty putting words to our internal experience, and that our problem-solving strategies are more introspective and mechanistic than women's.

I'm not about to suggest that a man's silence is due to a woman's behavior. No one bears responsibility for the way another person chooses to act. At the same time, both partners contribute to the patterns that evolve in their relationship—patterns that encourage them to respond in a way that seems useful in the moment, but may be counterproductive in the long run.

Why Women Should Accept Compliments

Men want to be effective in everything we take seriously, and that includes expressing our affection for the women we love. Women often fail to understand how frustrating it is when they argue with the compliments we offer. This is a common complaint from men. As one man put it, "Women tend to deny every compliment guys give, and it makes us want to stop giving them."

Refusing our compliments is remarkably frustrating. Imagine you bought a gift for your best friend. You wrapped it nicely and tried to give it to her, only to have her turn it down. "I'm not worth it," she says. You buy another gift, and she insists that you weren't thinking clearly. You buy another, and it too is refused. How long would it take you to give up?

We give compliments to show that we're paying attention to you and that you're important to us. Accepting the compliment may be uncomfortable, but nothing will make your partner happier in that moment than simply accepting what he has offered.

The Silence Hole

A lot of men do it. They do it after dinner; they do it in the car. They do it in bed, and they even do it when you're discussing your mother.

I'm talking about going silent, of course, and it seems that men are especially prone to silence during a conflict. She wants to talk, and he has checked out. I should point out that women sometimes retreat when men want to talk, but let's be honest: unwillingness to communicate is mainly a male behavior, and I admit that I struggle with it myself. You'd think a psychologist would know better, and in fact I do, but the old training to remain silent can be difficult to overcome at times.

Going silent is a behavior that can feed on itself until it seems to engulf the relationship. The natural response from many women is to force a conversation when their partner goes silent. Unfortunately, that can make it even more difficult for him to speak, which leads to more forcefulness, which leads to... Well, you get the picture.

In my previous book, I shared the story of Meg and Andy (Smith 2011). Their story is also relevant here, as they are poster children for couples who fall into the silence hole. Andy came from a home, where minor disappointments were often met with major punishment. As a kid, Andy learned to retreat to the safety of his bedroom whenever he sensed his unpredictable, alcoholic mother becoming angry. He's a somewhat extreme example, but most men find it terribly uncomfortable when the women in their lives are unhappy with them. It makes them anxious.

Whenever Meg got angry, Andy's anxiety led him to retreat and clam up—just as he had learned to do with his mother. He didn't do it to punish Meg. On the contrary, he was trying to prevent the problem from getting worse. For Andy, retreat was an old strategy that served him well in child-hood. But as an adult, his anxiety-ridden response created anxiety for Meg too. His silence made her worry about the relationship and ruminate about previous times he'd fallen silent, problems they had never solved, and the possibility that they would never be able to communicate. Meg tried to hold back her feelings, but eventually her concern for the relationship would become overwhelming. When she reached that breaking point, she'd corner Andy and vent her accumulated frustrations.

The irony of their situation is that each was trying, in his or her own way, to protect the relationship. Andy was trying to keep things from getting worse, figuring that an argument was the most destructive outcome possible. He tried to avoid arguing with Meg, hoping that the lack of arguments would make her happy. Meg, on the other hand, felt that not communicating about their problems was the worst possible strategy.

Andy's silent response achieved exactly what he was hoping to avoid: an angry wife. Meg's response also gave her an outcome completely at odds with what she wanted: a man who retreated further.

Good men aren't idiots. We know that silence makes things worse. So why do we do it? Let's look at a few of the more common reasons I've heard from men.

Men Ain't Supposed to Talk

As discussed in chapter 1, men are frequently at a disadvantage when putting words to emotions. During childhood development, girls tend to talk about relationships more than boys, so women are generally better trained in this skill. Putting men at an even greater disadvantage, many of us have been taught that it's effeminate to discuss...that stuff. As boys, we faced ridicule, bullying, or even punishment if we ventured too far toward what's seen as feminine discourse. Those experiences stay with us, often making us exceptionally anxious when we try to break old rules we've learned about gender.

We Feel We Cannot Win

A surprising number of men have admitted to me that they feel outmatched during arguments with their wives or girlfriends. They've said things like this:

* "I'm not as quick-witted as she is."

* "She comes prepared with her arguments, and I don't."

* "She seems to remember everything I've ever said or done. My mind doesn't work like that."

* "She brings up old arguments that I thought we'd settled. I don't know how to defend against that."

These men tend to believe that anything they say will get them into trouble. Talking makes them feel vulnerable to criticism or shame, so they do what seems like the only sensible thing: they stop talking.

We Get Angry

It's true, sometimes we clam up because we're angry. For many men, anger is the default response when we feel wounded, criticized, disrespected, isolated, or even sad. It often takes time for us to understand what has prompted our anger. Until we're ready to discuss it, retreat may seem to us like the only option that won't make things worse.

It Pains Us to Argue with You

A woman's unhappiness is a painful experience for many men.

There's an old stereotype that women care about relationships more than men. However, one study found that to be demonstrably wrong (Simon and Barrett 2010). Men care about relationships just as much as women, but in slightly different ways, and we're upset by different things. The researchers found that women tend to be more concerned about the status of the relationship—whether or not it feels secure. As a result, any instability in the relationship can have a deep, depressing effect on women's moods.

Men, on the other hand, are more troubled by relationship problems. Discord in a relationship damages our sense of worth, and sometimes even our health. So, whereas women have a tendency to respond to relationship instability with depression, men are more likely to respond to relationship discord with strategies like substance abuse. We react to relationship problems by retreating, avoiding, and self-destructing. Arguing with you literally hurts us.

When the same old arguments show up repeatedly, we start to feel incapable of keeping you happy. Eventually, some men give up and go silent because passively making things worse is more tolerable than speaking and actively making things worse.

History Drives Us

History was Andy's downfall. Despite his best intentions, he wasn't making well-informed decisions because his past was superimposing itself on his present. He was responding to Meg as if she were his mother—the angry, abusive woman he had lived with for so many years. As a child, he learned that conflict was dangerous and retreat was his safest response. His mind hadn't caught up to the fact that Meg was safe and kind, not abusive. Human minds often get stuck in the past like that.

When men bring the tendency to go silent into a relationship, it's tempting to respond by pushing harder to get them to talk, just as Meg did. As one woman told me, "Most of the time pushing men's buttons is the only way to get them to respond." Each time Meg responded with force, even with good intentions about saving the relationship, she helped strengthen a destructive pattern.

Transition Time

Because many men tend to compartmentalize their lives—work, home, recreation, and so on—they often need time to switch their mind-set from one environment to the next. Transitioning from work to home is a particular challenge. As one man explained, "The minute I get home from work isn't my favorite time for questions. I'd like to sit down for a few minutes before we go in depth on how my day went."

One of the exercises I suggest for men is to take a few moments before entering the next environment to remind themselves of the values and behaviors they want to manifest. One good way to do that is simply to ask this question: "What kind of man do I want to be when I get home (or arrive at work, arrive at the in-laws' house, and so on)."

For example, they might take a moment in the car before walking in the door after work, or both partners may agree to allow a man a certain period of time to transition to being home after they greet each other.

Here's how one man explained it: "We need just a little bit of time to gather ourselves, mostly when we get in the house, to flip the switch to home mode. If women subtly and gradually engage us instead of bombarding us, we can interact. We know that in today's age women have had just as hard a day as we have, and we want to come together with you, but sometimes responding to us quietly will go a lot further then swinging for the fences."

Problem Solving Versus Problem Behavior

The good news is that even troubling behavior like silence is often an attempt to solve a problem. In Andy's case, he was trying to protect Meg from disappointment. He was also trying to insulate her from an argument because, in his experience, arguments had always been miserable, with regrettable outcomes. He was simply trying to contain the situation before it got out of control, and, possibly because his anxiety was high, it didn't occur to him that Meg viewed his silence differently.

It might seem strange to think of Andy's silence as problem-solving behavior. However, in keeping with what will be a common theme in the rest of this book, I'm hoping to persuade you that recognizing a man's problem-solving behavior as such is one of the most useful things you can do for your relationship. But before we go forward, I want to make a clear distinction between problem-solving behavior and problem behavior.

Andy's silence was a hurtful behavior, but it wasn't dangerous, disrespectful, or abusive. Problem-solving behavior can be challenging to live with, emotionally hurtful, and even damaging to the relationship in the long run. But problem-solving behavior is never plainly abusive.

Problem-solving behavior doesn't involve name-calling, physical abuse, affairs, dishonesty, or hostility. Those are problem behaviors and should not be tolerated. If the man in your life is struggling to overcome problem behaviors, you should have an escape plan. If he has behavioral problems but isn't struggling to overcome them, perhaps it's time to explore the possibility of distancing yourself from him.

Fortunately, good men don't engage in major, repetitive problem behaviors. They may struggle with solutions that are ill suited to the situation, but they are not abusive. In chapter 7, I'll discuss specific ways to break patterns like the silence hole, but I need to lay some groundwork first. So in the next chapter, I'll discuss one of the greatest challenges between men and women: accepting our partners as they are.

For the Man in Your Life:
If the Hole Is Getting Deeper, Stop Digging

I couldn't afford to attend college straight out of high school. I had to work for a while and get established. One of my early jobs was as a pinsetter mechanic. Through a fortunate turn of events and solid mechanical aptitude, I found myself maintaining and repairing the machines that set pins and return balls at a large bowling alley. It was one of my favorite jobs.

Being a typical, cocky young guy, I had a tendency to take on repairs that were beyond my skill level. One time I tried to repair a broken table shaft—an expensive component central to the machine's ability to retrieve bowling pins from the deck and return them to their spots. This one had become fatigued and developed a nasty spiral crack. The effect on the machine was the same that of as a broken axel on a car. The senior mechanics said it was beyond repair and needed to be replaced.

I wagered that I could weld it back, good as new, despite the fact that the best welder in the shop said it was hopeless and my welding skills were middling at best. Over the course of a few weeks, I spent my odd moments trying to repair the part. But with each effort, the problem got worse. Eventually, I ended up hiding it in my locker and hoping no one would discover how badly I had mangled it.

My misplaced efforts made no difference. A new shaft was installed long before I realized that I was out of my depth. Nevertheless, I had developed a single-minded approach that wasted my time and the company's resources. With each attempt to fix the thing, I was digging the hole deeper, yet I couldn't bring myself to stop digging.

Because we men are fixers, we have a tendency to fall into the same trap in our relationships. This chapter began with the story of Oscar, a man named who was hell-bent on fixing problems for his wife and forged ahead even when his efforts were making things worse. Like me, Oscar didn't know when to stop digging.

If you're like a lot of guys, you may have noticed that you repeatedly experience the same problems with the woman you love. If so, there's every possibility that your approach to keeping her happy is backfiring and you don't yet understand how or why.

If that seems like a possibility, it might be time to evaluate your strategy, discuss the nature of the repetitive problems with her, and possibly even hire a shrink to help you stop digging. Only then can you identify the problem and implement a solution that works.

Chapter 6

The "A" Word

Acceptance is a bit like money. We're all happy to receive it, but doling it out can be anxiety provoking.

Earlier, I mentioned that I won't offer advice on how to change the nature of a man, nor will I suggest changing your nature to suit him. At first glance, that may seem to make it difficult to fix a relationship. After all, how can things improve if nobody changes?

But that's often the wrong question. It's true that change is sometimes necessary. Some men behave badly, and if they don't change their behavior, the relationship may never be healthy or tenable. But those aren't the men I'm talking about. In this book, I'm discussing good men with strong male natures. With good men, the more useful question is how you can incorporate male nature into a strong male-female partnership.

In so many relationships I hear women asking a different type of question: "How can I get him to change?" "How can I get him to start doing this?" "How can I get him to stop doing that?" Often, these questions can be boiled down to, "How can I get him to act more like a woman?"

Let me be clear: I think you should ask for what you want in a relationship. If your partner is leaving dirty socks on the floor for you to pick up, that's disrespectful behavior. He needs to know that, and he needs to change.

But couples don't turn to people like me to manage low-level sock problems. They're trying to repair serious rifts, and those rifts almost always have something to do with unwillingness to accept a partner's traits and characteristics.

This battle against acceptance often costs people their values. I haven't really discussed values yet, so let me take a brief aside. Think back to the time when you were a starry-eyed teenager with all of your romantic ideals intact. Back then, if I had asked you what kind of partner you wanted to be in a relationship, you might have said you wanted to be romantic, playful, or caring. You might have said you wanted to be capable of a deep, lifelong connection, or that you wanted to be the kind of person your partner would always be able to depend on. I know I would have said something like that.

Those qualities are your values. They describe the kind of person you want to be, not the kind of person you want your partner to be. Ideally, your values would guide your behavior, and your partner's values would guide his.

But values are tough to maintain. As life roughs us up, it's easy to lose track of our ideals and start behaving as if we must hide our values in order to protect ourselves, or to start feeling that the only way we can get our needs met is through coercive means. When that happens, a relationship can end up feeling more like a tug-of-war than a partnership.

Fighting our partner's nature rather than accepting it also tends to get us precisely what we least want. Here's a little experiment you can try right now. If I ask you not to think about monkeys, what's the first thing that comes to mind? Of course, it's monkeys.

Now suppose I asked you to work really, really hard at not thinking of monkeys. Suppose I asked you to devote your life to the act of not thinking about monkeys. I want you to become a no-monkey monk. If your mind is like most people's, monkeys will become the most important thing in your life (Wegner et al. 1987). Everything you do will be in the service of avoiding them, and therefore, in a strange way, your life will revolve around monkeys. You'll get precisely what you tried to avoid.

A similar thing happens in relationships. In each of the couples I've described so far, both the women and the men denied, fought, or tried to avoid dealing directly with male nature. As a result, some of the least useful aspects of male nature began to crowd out some of the most useful. The less willing both people were to embrace what they disliked about male nature, the more of it they got—just like the monkeys. There has to be an easier way.

An Intimidating Word

"Acceptance" can be a frightening word—threatening, even. Like most people, your mind may naturally go to worst-case scenarios: "You mean I have to accept his unkindness?" "I have to accept his bad behavior?" "I have to accept that our relationship will never be healthy?"

Absolutely not. Acceptance doesn't mean tolerating unhealthy relationships or problem behavior. In relationships, acceptance has two key qualities. First, it means being willing to recognize that your partner, right here and right now, is struggling too. It means allowing for the possibility that his motivations might be good and constructive, even if it doesn't feel that way. It means not getting caught up in the belief that he's wrong or doesn't care about you, and instead embracing the possibility that he's doing the best he can. He may even be trying to keep you happy—but in a way that only makes sense inside his male mind. Acceptance also means embracing the formidable task of empathizing with your partner's struggle when you least want to do so.

Second, it means being willing to embrace anxieties and insecurities within yourself. We tend to choose mates who ease our greatest

How Men Think

"When we fight, I can't think, sleep, or eat until there is resolution."

insecurities, like Samantha, who chose Tyrone partly for his confidence. That worked out well, until she began to feel that his assertiveness was impeding her self-expression. That was the point at which she started feeling as if his personality was a liability to the relationship, and she began struggling against the very trait she once found to be so attractive in him.

Have you or your partner ever asked, "What happened to you? Why did you change?" If so, there's a good chance that one or both of you has fallen into the trap of refusing to accept your partner's traits, or to recognize your own struggles against those traits. As soon as we start fighting against that which we can't change or control, we can lose track of our values. We become people we don't want to be. On the other hand, when we let go of the struggle and instead accept our partner's traits and our own, suddenly we have more time and energy to be who we want to be in the relationship. We get to be the person our partner fell in love with.

It can be frightening to stop believing our own judgments and drop our defenses. Fighting against perceived hurts has the appearance of keeping us safe. As long as Samantha was railing against Tyrone's assertiveness, she felt she was protecting herself. It can also be frightening to embrace male nature, for reasons I'll discuss shortly. But I've seen the result countless times: a good man will usually respond in kind when his partner accepts him for who he is. I'll discuss why shortly.

Acceptance of *both* of your natures and struggles is one of the greatest gifts you can give to a man—especially during those moments when you aren't in the gift-giving mood.

Still, acceptance can be intimidating. And yes, you might get hurt. For that reason, I don't want to talk you into it. I don't want you to try it just because I've seen it work out well. You should trust your own experience, not mine.

Maybe it's true that a woman who accepts the man in her life unconditionally, with all of his confounding male traits and quirks, will end up with more emotional pain rather than less. Maybe

> ## How Men Think
>
> **"The worst moments are when a woman is angry with me."**

embracing her own insecurities, rather than covering them over with well-practiced defenses, places her in jeopardy. But I think the only way to know for sure is to gamble on it. Of course, I can't advise you to gamble when I don't know what the stakes are. I can only ask, What is there to lose? That's an important question, so let's take a close look at it.

Reasons Not to Embrace Male Traits

Think back to one of the first couples we discussed, Sam and Tamara, from chapter 1. Sam retreated into his job when home life became stressful, and Tamara was unhappy. They ended up arguing over everything except the real issue, which was that, in the course of trying to be a good provider, Sam got his priorities out of balance.

As tensions mounted in the relationship, the ambition and sense of duty that Tamara once admired in Sam became the very qualities that were least acceptable to her. She came to resent the same male traits she once loved. In turn, Sam became defensive about those traits, and they fell into a pattern of avoidance and bickering rather than discussing his struggle. I want to emphasize that I'm not placing blame on Tamara. Sam avoided the discussion as much as she did—probably more so.

Acceptance feels risky, and let's be honest: sometimes it is. Some men use a woman's acceptance and tolerance as a license for bad behavior. But a good man will meet acceptance with acceptance, and usually with gratitude.

Still, it's the nature of the human mind to protect us from anything that might be dangerous. That's why the mind can hit us with scenarios of broken hearts and broken dreams when we begin to consider dropping our defenses and taking a riskier course, even if it's potentially more productive. Here are some of the common fears women have expressed to me about accepting their partner's male nature and traits:

* *The problem could escalate.* A lot of women fear that if they disengage from whatever tug-of-war they've fallen into with their partner, the problem will only get worse. For example, suppose a man doesn't call his wife or girlfriend frequently enough. She wonders where he is and what he's doing, worries about him, and feels disconnected. She may fear that if she stops pressuring him about this, he'll never call at all.

* *Accepting his nature is like admitting I'm wrong.* If a woman feels she must manage a man's behavior, reversing course can feel like an admission that he was right and she was wrong.

* *Acceptance will send the message that he doesn't need to fix anything.* Some women fear that if they stop trying to correct their partner's male nature, he may come to the mistaken conclusion that he's perfect just the way he is. Eventually, his slovenly, disorganized, or thoughtless behavior might consume the relationship.

* *If I accept him the way he is, I'll end up doing all the work.* If a woman sends the message that a man's traits are acceptable, he'll have no reason to work on improving the relationship.

He'll have no reason to take her out to dinner or to feed the baby in the middle of the night. She'll end up sacrificing her self-interests, compromising her values, and doing all the work in the relationship.

* *I'll discover what kind of man he really is, and I won't like it.* Some women fear that dropping the battle against their partner's male nature may unleash a flood of thoughtless, hurtful behaviors that no woman wants to see in her man.

A few other common fears are more complex, so I want to discuss them in greater detail.

Acceptance Means the Real Problem Won't Get Fixed

Consider a man who barely talks as it is. His partner may fear that if she stops fighting to fix the problem, he'll recede into the woodwork entirely. There is every possibility that accepting a man's nature will give him permission to act poorly, and perhaps even take advantage, but that depends on the man. If your partner interprets your acceptance as giving him license to devalue the relationship, the relationship has serious problems, beginning with a lack of mutual respect.

That's unfortunate, but it's also instructive. Perhaps it's better to know the truth so the two of you can respond honestly and directly to that serious problem. However, good men respond well to acceptance for a couple reasons.

First, acceptance of the way men think—the way they approach relationship problems, the way they think about themselves in relationships, and the ways in which male thinking can be useful in relationships—is unusual. Your partner is probably going to enjoy it, and he's probably going to want more of that kind of intimacy with you.

Second, good men want a good relationship and a happy partner. When their partners are happy, it usually makes men happy. That happiness is likely to translate into affection and willingness to make the relationship even better.

If it will be new behavior for you to embrace your partner's male style of thinking, communicate with him about it. Tell him about your intention to change your approach. You might say something like "Honey, I realize that I've been pushing you to change and it isn't working, so instead I'm going to work on understanding the way you think and accepting the different ways we approach things. Of course, my hope is that you'll return the effort, but I'm not doing it to manipulate you. I'm doing it to be the kind of person I want to be in our relationship."

I know those can be frightening words to say. It may be easier if both of you treat it as an experiment. If the acceptance experiment fails, you can always go back to your old ways—or better yet, use the new information to increase your understanding of the underlying problem.

Mistreatment Could Escalate

Some women fear that acceptance might mean problem behavior, such as drinking, cheating, or abusiveness, could get worse. If this is your concern, male nature isn't the issue, nor is acceptance. These are signs of serious problems. The first and primary concern is safety. If your partner's behavior poses any kind of threat, it's probably time to put down this book, seek safety, and enlist help.

Acceptance Means Giving Up Your Story About What's Wrong

A final issue, and one that's tough to come to grips with, is that accepting a man's nature may mean a woman has to embrace the possibility that she has somehow contributed to problems in the relationship.

Personally, facing up to the possibility that I'm contributing to a problem is one of my least favorite things to do. We all have our stories about our relationships and how they work, and we're often the heroes or victims in our own minds, depending on which serves us best.

In our society, it has become a common message, in everything from movies to advertisements, that men are inept in relationships. It's easy to buy into the idea that relationship problems begin and end with men. I've even seen members of my own profession do this, and not just the female shrinks.

Pinning relationship problems on male nature is an easy answer, and male nature means that men often accept the blame and try to change (though our attempts to change can be difficult to recognize). The trade-off for that convenience is that nobody ends up happy because destructive patterns continue, often showing up at the worst moments.

Most people don't want to be the first to change their behavior in a relationship. For many women, hesitating to accept male nature boils down to a fear that their partner won't care enough to respond in a thoughtful and loving way.

Room for Error

A man who took my survey described one of the most common dynamics that discourages men from trying to make women happy: "They don't forget anything. The old mistakes, the purchases that didn't work out, the words said in anger—a guy can never take them back. Women always bring them back up in an argument. They won't accept an apology and forget it."

Bringing up past events in an argument is often an attempt to gain reassurance that old problems won't be repeated in the future. It's a problem-solving strategy designed to eradicate painful patterns.

But to the man on the receiving end, it can seem pointlessly aggressive, and it can cause the discussion to devolve into unproductive bickering over particular events rather than problematic patterns.

If one partner in an argument (often the man) is focused on present events, and the other (frequently the woman) is focused on patterns and history, each person is trying to solve a different problem. The partner who's focused on patterns and history is likely to end up feeling unheard, and the one focused on the immediate problem is likely to fear forever being punished for past mistakes.

That's precisely the fear that many men have described to me. As one man explained it, "When you remember our past mistakes but forget our successes, we think you expect us to be perfect." This often compels men to retreat rather than face an impossible standard.

Men tend to feel more comfortable in discussions when we know the ground rules. Set some guidelines at the outset of a difficult conversation, and let your partner know whether you want to discuss the immediate problem, past patterns, or concerns about the future. Many men prefer to do one thing at a time. We can end up feeling discouraged or hopeless when we're chasing multiple problems at once and perceive that none of them are being solved.

Should You Change, or Should He?

It's easy and even satisfying to pin problems on our partner's nature. I think one of the things that makes it so temping is the fact that sometimes we're right. Sometimes it is the other person's fault. And sometimes men really are buttheads (as are women on rare occasion), so it may be easy to latch onto a few unfortunate samples of bad behavior and imagine that they represent your partner's true nature.

Here's an example: Rick once got drunk—a rare occurrence for him—and insulted his wife's mother. He didn't do it to her face; he called her a derogatory name in his wife's presence. In truth, he liked his mother-in-law. But on that occasion he was having difficulties with other people in his life, and he misdirected his anger.

The incident didn't cause any direct damage. His mother-in-law never heard the hurtful words. But from that moment on, his wife, Angie, assumed that his momentary lapse represented his true feelings.

When Rick was sober the next day, he tried to explain to Angie that his remarks didn't represent his feelings toward her mother, but it was too late. Despite years of evidence that he admired her mother, she had difficulty letting go of his comment. He couldn't convince her that it wasn't true.

She even took his denial as evidence, thinking, *He must hold that belief pretty deeply if he has to work that hard to hide it.* Angie's reaction is common. The mind will latch onto anything that seems the least bit threatening. Her difficulty letting go probably stemmed from a perceived threat to familial harmony. Still, she was refuting his nature based on a single incident, and that can snowball into real problems.

When Angie bought into the thought that Rick disliked her mother, she began to act as if he disliked her mother. She acted apologetically whenever Rick encountered her mother, and she tried to insulate them from each other. She was also nervous that Rick would insult her mother again, and that anxiety created a slightly awkward tone whenever Rick and her mother were together.

Angie's behavior didn't make Rick dislike her mother, but it did create a palpable distance between him and her mother. Angie's denial of his true feelings helped create exactly what she feared in him. It also made it impossible for Rick to please her in this realm, which was particularly hurtful to him.

This kind of dynamic can show up in many ways. For example, a man who fears that his wife is suspicious can begin to hide his activities, which will indeed evoke suspicion.

This dynamic definitely affected Tamara and Sam's relationship. Tamara believed that Sam was escaping into work because he didn't like her, so she began to act as if he didn't like her, even though he did. She certainly didn't cause his behavior, but by refuting Sam's nature and feelings and buying into her own story about him, Tamara unwittingly contributed to making their home atmosphere so unpleasant that Sam wanted to escape. In this way, she brought to life her own worst fears about Sam. And just like Angie, she made it increasingly difficult for her husband to please her—a position that most men dislike intensely.

So, based on an understanding of that dynamic, let's return to the question of which partner should change. If you think of Sam as a litigator would, you can make a pretty strong case that he was responsible for the relationship problems. He was the one who withdrew from the family. He was the one who put his coworkers before his wife. He disregarded Tamara's true needs. Clearly he's the one who should change.

But you could make an equally strong case that Tamara was at fault. She disregarded the difficulties Sam faced at work. She started nagging and became unpleasant to be around. She dug the hole deeper by adding pressure when Sam withdrew. Clearly she's the one who should change.

If it isn't obvious by now, I think "Should you change, or should he?" is, in most cases, a trick question and a false dilemma. There is a third option.

Embracing the Other Side of the Coin

The third option is simply to tackle problematic patterns as a team rather than trying to force one partner to change. Changing problematic patterns is more generally satisfying and productive than the alternative, and in the next chapter, I'll offer some guidance on how to do this. But in my experience, it's difficult for couples to focus on changing patterns when they're still caught up in the idea of changing each other.

Accepting our partners' nature—embracing it and welcoming it into the relationship—is somehow easier when we acknowledge that their most annoying traits are often the other side of the qualities we most admire. They're two sides of the same coin. The men whose stories I've shared each have what you might consider to be strong, stereotypically male traits, and each of those traits had a dark side:

* Mike was strong and stoic, but his stoicism created a rift in his relationship.

* Sam's desire to be a good provider separated him from his family.

* Tyrone's self-assuredness made him seem overbearing.

* Justin's reliance on his resourcefulness left his wife feeling as if he had no regard for the future.

* Oscar's desire to fix other people's problems made his wife and daughter feel disregarded.

    *   Andy's quest for a peaceful home created moments of intense conflict.

For all of them, their best and least useful male qualities were two sides of the same coin. Here's the question that each of us in a relationship must face: Can you travel with those coins lightly in your pocket, each holding the potential for both joy and pain?

Hopefully I've made the case that embracing male traits can open the door to possibilities that have seemed unattainable. Doing so may allow you to productively change patterns in your relationship rather than unproductively battling against your partner's male nature—a nature that can be a strong and wonderful ally.

We've come to the end of our journey with Mike, Sam, Tyrone, and the other men discussed in parts 1 and 2 of the book. In part 3, we'll focus on how to communicate with the less communicative gender.

For the Man in Your Life:
Know What Kind of Armor You Wear

Guys, let's talk about secondary emotional reactions. They are emotions that cover up an initial emotional reaction, like feeling disappointment on the inside but showing anger on the outside. Most men have been trained to hide emotions that make us look like wimps, so we disguise them with manly displays of anger, humor, withdrawal, and the like. For most men, the process is so automatic that we don't even realize we're doing it.

Secondary emotional reactions make us look and feel strong, but they come at a cost. They can leave the women in our lives feeling frustrated, angry, hurt, or isolated. No good man sets out to accomplish that.

Any man who wants a happier relationship needs to familiarize himself with his own secondary reactions. I, like many men, am quick to anger. But that anger is usually covering up a "softer" emotional response, like the fear that I'm about to be disappointed or the pain of being treated disrespectfully. Sometimes those injuries exist only in my imagination, but my secondary reactions come on line as if they were real. Recognizing my secondary reactions for what they are—a mask—helps me respond thoughtfully rather than going off half-cocked.

Understanding your own secondary reactions isn't rocket science. It's a matter of reviewing a slow-motion replay of internal events. If you want to do that quickly and efficiently, hire a shrink. A good one will get the job done right. If you're not up for that, writing about what happens inside your head is another useful strategy.

That's right, I said writing, as in journaling. A few minutes here and there—especially after experiencing rough emotions—will help you understand what's going on under the hood. You don't have to write longhand. You can do it on a computer, and you can lock the file down like Fort Knox so no one else will see it. Journaling is useful because it requires you to process information verbally, and it's a fairly efficient way to understand your inner workings and prevent the same old problems from repeating.

Secondary reactions are like emotional armor. They can protect you up to a point, in the same way that a roll cage can protect a driver. But roll cages and armor are short-term solutions. It's better to avoid crashing and burning in the first place. That requires insight, and insight takes practice.

Part 3

How to Speak Manese

There are horse whisperers, dog whisperers, and even cat whisperers. They learn to speak the language of animals rather than depending on animals to learn the language of people. That two-way communication creates a supremely peaceful relationship. A skill like that might even come in handy between the genders. I suppose a woman who learned the language of men could be considered a "man whisperer."

Women tend to be skilled with words and emotions. Men don't lead with these; they aren't our strong suit. Yet in relationships, men are often asked to repress their greatest competencies and instead rely upon the very words and emotions that can be so elusive.

That's a fair thing to ask of men, but it's effective only up to a point. What if women and men met each other halfway, combining the verbal and emotional skills of women with the enthusiastic problem-solving skills of men? Combining the best of both could make you a certified man whisperer.

Chapter 7

Break the Pattern,
Not the Man

Here's one of the more destructive and common sentiments a woman can bring into a relationship: *If you loved me, you wouldn't act that way.* This can show up in many guises: *You wouldn't be so stoic. You wouldn't spend your Sundays watching sports. You wouldn't avoid my family. You wouldn't spend so much time at work.*

Statements like those are usually intended to get reassurance about a man's love. They may even work sometimes, but often they create the opposite of loving feelings. It's destructive for a couple of reasons.

First, it contradicts and invalidates what the man probably feels—he does love his partner, *and* he likes to watch sports. If a woman repeatedly accuses her man of not loving her, he may begin to believe it because it's such a discouraging thing to hear from the woman to whom he has devoted himself.

Second—and the topic of this chapter—this false dichotomy ("If you loved me you wouldn't...") is a grand diversion from whatever is really happening in the relationship. I've seen it countless times in my own practice: as soon as a woman utters that variety of sentiment, the couple gets sucked into an argument over whether or not the man has sufficiently demonstrated his devotion:

Her: Sometimes I think that if you really loved me, you'd want to spend more time with me.

Him: That's ridiculous. If I didn't love you, I wouldn't have married you! And we do stuff together all the time. I didn't even complain when you dragged me to that stupid coed baby shower last week.

Her: You only went because you knew I'd be mad if you didn't.

Him: Oh, give me a break! I do everything you ask me to do.

Her: Yeah, and you pout every step of the way!

And so on. It's like a relationship wormhole that sends a couple to a distant galaxy with slim chances of ever getting home. It's exhausting and endless, and neither person comes out feeling good.

The real issue often boils down to something like this: the woman feels lonely and her partner feels unable to please her, so they fall into this natural trap. Unfortunately, anytime one partner invokes "If you loved me…," the other will be on the defensive. A man on the receiving end of that phrase might eventually conclude that there's no way to please his partner.

No-win situations are devastating to relationships. To illustrate that painful fact, let's look at a more detailed example. Then I'll discuss how to avoid putting men in no-win situations.

• Tim and Julie

Tim and Julie were in their midthirties when they married, and it was the second marriage for each of them. Tim said his first wife divorced him because she was never happy: "Maybe we just weren't meant to be together. It seemed like I could never do enough for her or be the right kind of guy for her."

Julie's first marriage was also unpleasant: "I never could fully trust my first husband. I know he had a girlfriend on the side from the beginning. Maybe he cleaned up his act, but I always had the sense that he was hiding something. We were constantly fighting over where he was and what he was doing."

How Men Think

"She can turn anything into an argument. Once she's upset at me, there's no escape."

Not long after their respective divorces, Tim and Julie fell in love. Coming from bad marriages, both were hungry for affection and closeness, and also hungry to care for someone else without the judgments and suspicions that had tormented them in their previous relationships. In the early days of their relationship, everything seemed so simple and joyous. They felt so simpatico.

Sadly, every honeymoon phase comes to an end. Several months into their marriage, Tim began to be drawn toward his work and away from Julie. His intent wasn't to ignore or withdraw from her, but simply to restore what felt like lost balance. He had enjoyed the honeymoon phase, but he saw it as just that—a phase—and felt it was time to start focusing on work again.

In typical male fashion, Tim didn't communicate that insight to Julie. He assumed she must feel the same way, especially because their thoughts and feelings had always been so in sync.

But to Julie, it felt as though Tim was ever so subtly slipping away. She noticed that he was spending extra hours at work, that he was less affectionate than before, and that he sometimes seemed preoccupied. Those shifts in his time and attention awakened old anxieties for her. The last time she'd felt a man's affection slipping away, it was the beginning of a long and painful decline in the relationship, which ended in divorce. Julie tried to resist her doubts, but her anxiety led her to question Tim's devotion. She started asking him what he was doing, why he was spending less time with her, and when he'd be able to spend more time together again.

These were all perfectly reasonable questions, and Tim should have been able to answer them with his equally reasonable explanation. He should have been able to tell Julie that he loved her as much as ever. Had he responded that way, they probably could have had a loving and productive conversation about the time they spent together.

But as with Julie, Tim's anxiety got the better of him. When she began to question him, his mind flashed back to his first wife—the woman he could never satisfy, who ultimately left him. So he gave Julie terse answers. Once when she called him at work to find out when he'd be home, he brusquely replied, "I'm working. I'll be home when I'm done." To Julie, it seemed as if he was angrily brushing her off. In truth, he was simply nervous and hoped a firm response would show her that he wouldn't be pushed around.

The situation rapidly escalated into a cycle that was painful for both of them. The more Julie pushed for reassurance of Tim's love, the more he resisted. The more he resisted, the more she pushed. Before long, their exchanges became heated, with Julie saying things like "I don't know why I bother trying to talk to you. You always run away!" and Tim shooting back angry responses, such as "Maybe you should just get off my back once in a while!"

Eventually, they reached an impasse where Tim avoided almost any conversation about their relationship and Julie felt as though she was constantly chasing him and digging for scraps of information and affection. It felt a lot like her first marriage, where she was always starved for information and fearful that a conversation would turn ugly without warning.

It was equally painful for Tim. Just as in his first marriage, he felt as if there was no way to keep his wife happy. He felt he had failed at love once again. He and Julie could hold civil conversations about trivial things and they even enjoyed each other's company much of the time, but he dreaded the possibility that the conversation might turn toward something deeper. That fear almost made him want to avoid Julie altogether, and he wondered how things ever got so bad.

Spotting a Pattern

I chose Tim and Julie's story for a couple of reasons. First, they had fallen into a pattern of retreat and pursuit, with Tim avoiding conversations and Julie chasing him down. This may be one of the most common relationship patterns that can be traced almost directly to differences in male and female nature. Second, since the male way of thinking contributes to the pattern, it gives us a good chance to look at how men think.

Before a couple can break a pattern, they first have to notice that it exists. That sounds obvious, right? Unfortunately, noticing patterns turns out to be one of those skills that's easier said than done. In fact, if I were writing a dictionary of relationships, I'd define a relationship pattern as a set of repetitive behaviors that couples frequently stop noticing.

In part, this happens because emotions get in the way. For example, Tim was beginning to feel fear and frustration about failing in a relationship again. Whenever a heavy discussion seemed imminent, this oppressive fear, which remained unrecognized and unnamed, pushed him in a safe direction, away from the painful conversation.

Couples also get blinded to patterns because it's so easy to get caught up in minute incidents rather than the emotional wounds they cause. Tim and Julie could have spent days arguing about his work schedule without acknowledging the pain each of them felt. As UCLA psychology professor Andrew Christensen told me in conversation, couples often become fixated on the arrow, not the wound. However, it's generally more productive to talk about the emotional vulnerability than the incident that sparked it.

I spoke with Christensen about patterns like the one Tim and Julie fell into—a pattern so common that researchers have given it a name: the demand-withdrawal pattern. He told me that the role each partner takes in the demand-withdrawal pattern depends upon their stakes within the relationship at any given time. For example, if a man wants sex and a woman doesn't, then he's in the demand role and she's withdrawing. He said women typically find themselves in the demand role because they often want a higher level of togetherness than men. Women also seek improvements in relationships more frequently than men, which Christensen believes is one of the reasons women initiate couples therapy more often.

Of course, men also want closeness, though the closeness they desire may look different. One man told me, "Men are simple, direct people who desire warmth and intimacy." Another said, "We mostly try to hide our emotions. That doesn't mean we don't have feelings; we just choose to not show them any more than we have to."

Although both genders want intimacy, Christensen believes that it makes sense that women are more often in the role of demanding emotional closeness. For most of our species's history, women have needed a more nurturing relationship for protection during vulnerable times, such as pregnancy and childbearing. Men, on the other hand, had less at stake emotionally and needed less contact. (I think it's also noteworthy that men were frequently engaged in team-based activities, away from home, that contributed to the survival of women and children.) It's easy to imagine how our ancestors developed the demand-withdrawal pattern and handed it down to us.

However we arrived at the current state of things, Christensen has found that although men often withdraw from conflict as a way to avoid problems, it's a terrible experience for women. As he told me, "Men often don't realize how painful their withdrawal is, thinking, *If we're not getting along, let's just avoid each other and not talk.* That seems like such a straightforward solution, whereas for women, or anyone who's wanting more connection, it can be a very painful outcome."

Giving Him a Way to Win

In my experience, many couples try to solve problems by focusing on single events rather than larger patterns. Like Tim and Julie, they can get lost down the rabbit hole, arguing about specific incidents and becoming increasingly oblivious to the fact that they are having the same old argument with different incidentals. For example, whether they were arguing about Tim's work schedule or his time with friends, Julie was probably thinking something like this: *If we can figure out why he's spending more time away from me, maybe we can stop the problem. Maybe he'll realize how hurt I feel, and we can be close again.* And Tim's thinking was probably along these lines: *I wish she would realize that I love her. If I can just put an end to this argument, maybe we can be close again.*

Here's a not-so-secret tip about human nature: we don't switch strategies easily. When an approach doesn't work, men and women alike tend to try harder with ineffective strategies. In relationships, that can easily result in fixating on the wrong thing. By focusing on the arrow of working longer hours, Tim and Julie lost sight of the wounds: Julie felt abandoned, and Tim felt criticized and inadequate. That's their demand-withdrawal pattern, and that's what they need to discuss.

You might be thinking, *Yeah, right. My partner isn't about to start discussing his emotions.* You may be correct, but in my experience most men are more willing to talk about patterns than about their personal or behavioral shortcomings, for more than one reason.

First, a pattern is an identifiable problem that a man can sink his teeth into. A common fear among men is that every argument is a losing proposition for them. As one man told me, "Men want to remove the guesswork. We want to know that there *is* a right answer." Focusing on a pattern, rather than specific events, gives a man hope that the problem can be solved. This man said it bluntly, but I think he described how many men, unfortunately, end up thinking about their partners: "I think guys would be more inclined to communicate if women were more willing to get to the point and fix the problem rather than avoid the solution and focus on the symptoms."

It may seem odd to hear a man complaining about women avoiding solutions when so many women feel it is men who avoid talking. But this is, in fact, how many men feel when a problem shows up repeatedly without resolution. They begin to think that women are more interested in perpetuating problems than solving them.

The second reason men are typically more willing to focus on patterns rather than specific events or shortcomings is because it sends a message of shared responsibility. It tells a man that he won't be under attack. Men often feel that they're being blamed for relationship difficulties and that there's no way to escape that blame. Focusing on patterns can avoid creating the sense of incompetence or hopelessness that drives them to retreat.

Noticing patterns isn't all that complicated, though it can be difficult to step away from specific events—the arrows—and notice the repetitiveness of the wound. If you're wondering whether you and your partner have fallen into a destructive pattern, consider whether either of you has ever said these kinds of things:

> ## How Men Think
>
> **"I want her to be happy, and I'm frustrated that easily fixed problems are treated as unsolvable crises. Really, I just want peace at home and that, for better or worse, is defined by my wife."**

* "Why do you always do that to me?"

* "Why do we have the same fights over and over?"

* "That was years ago. Why do you keep bringing it up?"

If so, there's a good chance that a pattern has taken hold. Noticing the pattern can be the hardest part. Once it's out in the open—meaning you've attached words and observations to it—its inner workings typically become more apparent. A good therapist can also help a couple stop launching arrows and start healing wounds.

You may wonder what comes next, after the pattern is out in the open and you've begun to identify how it works. Well, in the mangineering world, there's only one answer: fix it.

Changing the Pattern

Before I talk about improving a destructive pattern, let me give you an example of making a pattern worse. That's what happened to Esther, who brought her husband, Ethan, to therapy because she felt she couldn't trust him. She worried that he was carousing, womanizing, and doing all the things that bad boys do.

Her suspicions often led to heated arguments in which she pressed him to explain his whereabouts and activities and no answer he offered could satisfy her. No matter how thorough his explanations, her mind always seized upon perceived gaps in his story, causing her to interrogate him further. She grilled him about specific dates, times, and incidents. They could spend hours arguing over minutiae. Esther was always on the offense during these discussions, and Ethan was always on the defense. They were focused on a thousand little arrows, and never the wound.

The truth is, Esther's husband had given her reason to distrust him in the past, and that sparked a seed of suspicion that eventually consumed their relationship. Although Ethan had atoned for his transgressions and made substantial changes to his behavior, Esther's ongoing interrogations made him feel as if she would never forgive him. He eventually became so resentful about her accusations that he began to hide his behavior, sometimes disguising his whereabouts, despite the fact that he was doing nothing wrong. He was trying to protect his dignity, and in the process he behaved as if he were still untrustworthy.

Changing a pattern can be quite uncomfortable. Laying the groundwork for significant change in a relationship often means offering the other person precisely that which is least appealing to give. In Esther's case, that would have meant acting as if she trusted Ethan after she decided to forgive him. That may seem an unfair thing to ask. Why should Esther demonstrate trust when Ethan had been untrustworthy in the past? Why should it fall to her to clear a path to happiness?

If this were a book written to men, I'd be challenging them to a different but equally difficult task, as I routinely do in my practice, and as I'll do in the section for men at the end of this chapter. In this case, though, I'd offer the challenge to Esther, without coercion, and of course the choice would be entirely hers.

Because men so often feel as if they are less skilled than women at relationships, it's important to find the position that will help your partner lower his defenses. Should Esther have trusted her husband? It's not for me to say. I suppose it depends on whether she believed his changes were genuine. Offering trust to a transgressor puts a person in a vulnerable position, and I don't know whether Ethan deserved her trust.

But I can say with certainty that Esther and Ethan had fallen into a communication pattern similar to Tim and Julie's. They were caught up in the minutiae and unable to solve a larger problem because they focused on fleeting examples. Esther would question Ethan's whereabouts, Ethan would offer a defensive answer, and Esther would meet his defensiveness with more suspicion. It was exhausting, and it wasn't the relationship Esther wanted. She was losing sight of her relationship values.

Esther's alternative to acting in a way that increased Ethan's defensiveness—and this is the challenge—would be to offer something that helped him lower his defenses. That might mean dropping the battle for affection and togetherness and instead allowing Ethan to demonstrate affection when he chose and in his own way.

It may be helpful to discuss displays of affection with your partner so you'll be able to recognize them when they show up because, as we've discussed, men are sometimes coy in their expressions of love. Something as unromantic as fixing a leaky faucet may hold more meaning for him than for you.

Extending yourself to your partner in these ways may sound challenging, even threatening. There's a possibility that he might not reciprocate. But in general, a good man will happily return the effort when he sees a clear path to a peaceful relationship.

As Challenging as 1-2-3

Once we're caught in a tug-of-war like Esther's or Julie's, it's difficult to see anything but the rope. But couples in these situations have more options than they may realize. They don't have to stay stuck in painful patterns.

Below, I'll outline a simple (but challenging) recipe to help you and your partner create new and healthy patterns. Before you give it a try, one caveat: once you've decided to let go of the struggle at your end, explain that to your partner and extend a peace offering.

For Julie, that peace offering might sound something like this: "Tim, I realize that I've been trying to get more intimacy from you, trying to force you to spend more time with me. I realize that what I'm doing is only making things worse for us. I haven't been acting like the person I want to be in our relationship, so I'm going to start being less demanding and more loving."

For Esther, it might sound like this, "Ethan, I've been having trouble trusting you, so I've been acting as if you're untrustworthy. That's only making things worse for us, and it isn't the kind of partner I want to be. From now on, I'm going to try to act in a more trusting manner."

These are challenging things to say. In fact, these kinds of statements are likely to make you feel vulnerable to the very injuries you're trying to avoid. There are no guarantees of emotional safety. There is only his character upon which to base the decision.

Now here's that mangineering recipe for changing destructive patterns:

1. Notice when the pattern is reasserting itself.

2. Interrupt the pattern.

3. Replace the behavior.

1. Notice When the Pattern Is Reasserting Itself

Once you have made your peace offering, you and your partner should have a conversation about the pattern that has cropped up.

Julie might start the conversation with something like "I notice that whenever I start to feel like you don't want to be with me, I become insistent that you spend·more time with me. That seems to drive you away."

Esther might say something like, "I've noticed that when I begin to feel insecure about trusting you, I press you for details. That seems to make it harder for you to talk to me."

Both women could ask that in the future, whenever either partner begins to experience those old feelings cropping up (when Esther feels suspicious and insecure, when Julie feels lonely, or when their men feel the need to pull away), they identify the pattern, as it's happening, by putting words to the experience. Identifying the pattern as it's beginning to reappear is a vitally important step. Without identifying and labeling it, a couple is likely to be sucked back into it.

2. Interrupt the Pattern

The next step is to stop that old, habitual interaction as soon as the pattern begins to appear. Think of the warning lights on a car's dashboard. They alert you that something is wrong, but they don't necessarily tell you exactly what the problem is. The thoughts and feelings that show up at the beginning of the pattern are like those warning lights.

For example, Esther might notice the feeling that she can't trust Ethan or become aware of thoughts that he's doing something dishonest. Ethan might experience a flash of anger when he feels he's being interrogated or notice the thought that he can't get a break and Esther will always mistrust him. Those feelings and thoughts are their warning lights: *Don't keep driving. It's time to stop and check the engine.*

It's vital to discuss and identify those warning signs, to put words to them, so you each know when they appear. Most couples find that as soon as they notice the warning signs, it helps immensely to take a break and return to the conversation after an agreed-upon amount of time has elapsed. This gives both parties a chance to develop a more measured response. Don't be surprised if your partner needs more time than you to put words to his experience.

3. Replace the Behavior

When you return to the conversation—and it's important that you both agree beforehand to do so—discuss the wounds before you discuss the arrow.

For example, Julie might start the conversation like this: "When you said you couldn't leave work on time, I had the thought that you don't love me enough to want to be with me." Esther might say, "When I didn't know where you were during on your lunch break, I had the thought that I couldn't trust you."

At that point, your partner's job is to address the wound, not argue about the arrow. It's helpful to discuss that strategy beforehand, when you aren't in the emotional grip of the pattern. Explain that when you come to him with an effort to break the pattern, you'll be looking for him to acknowledge how you feel, not drag you back into the argument. Similarly, it will be helpful for him to identify his reaction and for you to acknowledge it.

For example Tim might say to Julie, "Yeah, when you seemed upset, I guess I had the urge to end the conversation. But I do love you and I want to spend time with you." Don't be afraid to coach your partner beforehand on the type of wording that will help you and help break the pattern. You may not want to offer that level of coaching because it might make it seem less meaningful when he uses the words. That's perfectly natural, but it's the kind of thing that can make men feel as if there's no path to happiness. It can feel as if you've hidden the key to your heart.

Sometimes we don't know what makes you happy unless you tell us. That isn't necessarily a reflection on our feelings for you. It may reflect nothing more than the different ways in which men and women express affection.

Why Men Don't Read Instructions

I'm like most guys when it comes to instruction manuals. I try to work it out on my own, and I only refer to instructions as a last resort.

It starts in childhood. Boys typically learn by experimenting and manipulating things in the physical world. It's part of the male mind's introspective, individualistic approach to problem solving, discussed earlier in the book.

This matters in relationships because it can make it look like men are unconcerned with relationship problems, when in fact many men spend a great deal of time thinking about their relationships. If you follow a group of men around a golf course, you'll hear these concerns—sparsely interspersed, of course, between conversations about business, cars, and good Scotch.

However, we don't necessarily approach our relationship problems by going to the bookstore to purchase a relationship instruction manual. We tend to approach relationship issues like any other problem: we experiment to figure out what works. This is why many men fall into a pattern of silence or withdrawal. Withdrawal reduces conflict. It restores order. It works.

Of course, it doesn't work *well*. Withdrawal is a temporary fix, and men know that. Most men, given the chance, will opt for long-term solutions to relationship problems, which is why I suggest a problem-solving approach that incorporates a bit of what men are good at: identifying systemic problems and eradicating them.

Men are great at fixing holes in roofs, bugs in software, and rattles in engines. Why not use those skills to improve relationships too?

What If He Doesn't Follow Your Lead?

Many men have told me that they feel at a verbal disadvantage with the women in their lives. They complain that they don't think as quickly during arguments or that their partners remember relationship history more easily. However, these same men often have good insights into the patterns in their relationships. Given the chance and a male-friendly strategy, most men are willing to work hard to improve their relationships.

But it is possible that the 1-2-3 approach could fail, or that your partner might use it to avoid dealing with problems in the relationship, for example, by never returning to the conversation after a planned time-out.

Also, be aware that trying to change patterns can reveal other issues or create new difficulties, at least in the short term. You may uncover resentful feelings that one of you had kept hidden, or learn that your problems are so entrenched that it's difficult to handle things more constructively. You may also find that your partner doesn't have the same degree of investment in improving the relationship as you do.

Personally, I prefer to have problems out in the open so I can find a new way to approach them, even if the problem seems discouraging. However, not everyone feels that way. Plus, not every little problem need not necessarily be brought into the light of day. This is something to consider before approaching your partner in a way that might expose his true feelings. There may be more under the surface than either of you realize.

Before the two of you embark on efforts to change your patterns, I recommend that you have a frank discussion about the possibility of unpleasant side effects. That said, I've rarely seen a pattern change turn out poorly. Even though changing patterns can be painful or challenging at first, in the end it's likely to improve the relationship.

For the Man in Your Life:
Be Impeccable

This chapter was about patterns that crop up repeatedly in relationships. Here's an example: Your partner wants the two of you to go to dinner with friends, and you tell her you have to work late. She says, "You never want to spend time with me," and the same old argument that you've had a thousand times is off and running.

In this chapter, I challenged your partner to break that kind of repetitive pattern. I asked her to do the one thing she may least want to do when that old argument starts up: consider your needs at the very moment when she feels that you are ignoring hers. (That's a tall order for anyone.) I also challenged her to rely a bit more on your skills and to trust that you'll rise to the occasion if she puts her faith in you.

Now I want to challenge you to help her. This chapter was about approaching relationship problems in a way that's more friendly to men: relying on fewer words and more action.

You know what? Why don't you just read the chapter. I'll wait here. Done? Great.

If the woman in your life is willing to try a different approach—one that puts her in a vulnerable spot—it's your job to keep her safe. The worst thing you could do to her, and to yourself, is to let her take that risk with the promise that you'll support her and then let her down by failing to keep your word.

If the two of you decide try what I've suggested in this chapter, she may ask you to do things differently, for example, going to your separate corners for an hour when an argument starts and then returning ready to discuss what you were thinking and feeling. She might even ask you to use that insightful male brain of yours to identify the systemic problems that are causing the relationship engine to rattle.

Don't agree to those actions unless you're willing to keep your word or die trying. Don't force her to distrust you when she's trying to improve your life together.

Do yourself a favor and be impeccable in your words and actions. I think the key to impeccability is staying on top of the little things before they become big things. If you say you're going to build a shelf, then build the shelf. If you say you're going to take a break from an argument and return in an hour, then do it. Some of the happiest, most relaxed women are the ones who know from experience that their partner is a man who keeps his word, even on the little things.

Chapter 8

Behind the Scenes

Men tend to leave women wondering what's really going on behind secondary emotional reactions—the reactions that appear on the outside to mask what's happening on the inside. Imagine a man who gets angry when trying to repair his car. On the inside, he might be feeling disappointment in himself or frustration because the task is interfering with his day. He may hide those thoughts and feelings behind anger directed outward: *What idiot engineer hid the battery compartment behind the quarter panel? You might as well bury it under a slab of concrete!* We men tend to mask our innermost thoughts and feelings behind a generous layer of manliness. *No kidding*, you might be thinking.

Because we men are so practiced at hiding our emotions, it's tempting to believe that we experience emotions to a lesser degree than women. Or maybe it would be more accurate to say that women have an unfair reputation for being overly emotional. The truth is, men's emotions are quite similar, though we often express them differently. Women aren't overly emotional (how would you define that, anyway?), nor are men unfeeling.

However, there are some subtle distinctions in the way men and women experience emotions. For example, men and women experience emotions like shame slightly differently, but the differences are much smaller than one might think (Else-Quest et al. 2012). And even though those emotional experiences are slightly different for men and women, the intensity is similar.

I know of no reliable evidence suggesting that men experience a lesser degree of primary emotions, such as sadness, joy, or fear, than women. The fact that we hide these things doesn't mean we don't experience them. Men are less expressive partly because we're socialized to be stoic (Kring and Gordon 1998). Our training in stoicism also makes us well practiced at secondary reactions.

With that as background, let's look at Gina and Brett's story. They're engaged in a common and destructive relationship pattern. But rather than focusing on the relationship pattern, as we have been, let's focus on what's going on behind the scenes for Brett.

• Gina and Brett

Gina and Brett met when they were fresh out of college and working their first jobs at an accounting firm. Brett first expressed his romantic interest by bringing coffee to Gina one morning. He had noticed her unusual habit of using honey in her coffee, and she was impressed that he mastered the ratio on the first attempt. That made Brett feel great.

As they began dating, Brett took great joy in doing small favors for Gina to make her job and her life easier. These little acts of service made him feel quite good. Brett's upbringing had left him rather insecure about his worth, and he'd discovered that serving others was a convenient way to get reassurance about his value as a person. He wasn't entirely aware that he was compensating for low self-esteem, but he knew that being useful somehow relieved a bit of anxiety.

He also enjoyed Gina's response to his favors. She was sweet and exceptionally appreciative of his efforts. She enjoyed hiding thank-you notes in his desk and sending him romantic, sometimes steamy text messages. Gina's upbringing had also left her insecure about her worth, so Brett's doting attention filled her need for reassurance every bit as much as it filled his desire to be valued. Gina returned the effort by doing favors for Brett sometimes, but early in their relationship a pattern developed in which he was more attuned to her needs than she was to his.

Brett and Gina eventually married and had a child. By then, their pattern had taken on an entirely different flavor. Gone were the honey-sweetened coffees and steamy thank-you notes. As the relationship matured, the little rituals that had once meant so much gave way to the demands of life. They simply had less time for their former romantic gestures, or failed to make time for them. Whatever the case, they found themselves in repeated conflicts that were ironic counterparts to the patterns of their early relationship.

Most confusing to Gina was Brett's range of contradictory responses. For example, once when she asked him to do her the small favor of putting gas in her car, he became visibly frustrated. He later said his reaction was a result of fatigue and a hard day at work, but she sensed there was something else behind his frustration.

On another occasion, she suggested that they forgo Christmas presents to each other in order to save money. He initially agreed and appeared to be glad about the decision, but within a few days he became sullen and withdrawn. "Why bother having Christmas at all?" he mumbled sarcastically when the topic resurfaced.

Those mixed signals left Gina feeling confused and isolated. She sensed an ambivalence in Brett's desire to please her that hadn't existed before. She became withdrawn, and she found it hard to trust his motives on the increasingly rare occasions when he went out of his way to please her like he used to.

In fact, Brett did feel ambivalent about trying to please Gina, but it wasn't because his love for her was fading. He felt that, somewhere along the line, Gina started taking him for granted. He wasn't sure how or when, but it seemed as if she felt entitled to his attention rather than appreciative of it.

As is often the case, Brett's perceptions probably had more to do with himself than with Gina. His need to be needed predisposed him to feeling unappreciated. Gina had become accustomed to his doting, but she found it difficult to maintain her previous levels of gushing appreciation as the honeymoon phase wore off. So Brett began to withhold favors in response to what he viewed as a lack of appreciation. When he began to withdraw his attention, Gina began to request more of it. And, as you've seen, these patterns can take on a life of their own.

Eventually, they fell into a kind of power struggle in which Gina pressed Brett to be the doting partner he once was and he dodged her requests. Both wanted to feel loved and appreciated as they once had, but Brett's responses left Gina feeling increasingly confused. When she asked him to run an errand or help her with a chore, he might respond in any number of ways. He might willingly comply, he might become visibly frustrated, or he might passively ignore the request, like the time she asked him to attend a work function with her and instead he scheduled a poker game with his friends without answering her request.

And just as Brett's insecurities predisposed him to feeling unappreciated, Gina's insecurities predisposed her to feeling unloved. Frustration sometimes overtook her, and she began to act, in Brett's words, "demanding and high-maintenance" as she tried to dissect his reactions.

Those "high-maintenance" moments occurred when Gina's confusion overtook her and she would corner Brett into relationship discussions that, to him, felt like grueling inquisitions.

She wanted to know why he no longer liked to do things for her and why he was hot and cold with her. She began questioning the minutiae of his behavior in an effort to reconcile the contradictions.

Those conversations ended with Brett walking away feeling defeated. Privately, he was as frustrated as Gina that he couldn't explain his behavior. In their more tender moments, he insisted that he still loved her. But the more she tried to express her needs, understand him, and connect with him, the more he responded in ways that didn't make sense to either of them.

The Stage Metaphor

Most good men lead a double life of sorts because hiding their feelings helps them succeed in life. Maybe it begins in childhood, when we learn not to cry in front of others. Maybe our group-focused predisposition teaches us to protect our reputation by not burdening others with our emotions. Maybe we just like to look tough to protect ourselves. Maybe it's all of the above combined with each man's unique history.

However it arises, most men learn early in life to maintain compartmentalized selves. It's like we're actors on a stage. We show the world—the audience that scrutinizes us—a well-rehearsed version of ourselves. Our purpose is to be as effective and successful as possible, even if it's all an act sometimes.

Backstage, it's a different story. Behind the controlled presentation, our minds can be bustling with activity. We keep our real emotional machinations—our sadness, disappointments, and vulnerabilities—hidden from view. On stage, for the world to see, we place our secondary emotional reactions—the anger, withdrawal, humor, or stoicism that we can safely present. As in a well-crafted stage play, the goal is to ensure that the audience never sees the orchestrations behind the production.

Sometimes we get so good at masking what goes on behind the scenes that we lose track of it ourselves. In large part, that's what happened to Gina and Brett. Because Brett was only partially aware of his need to be needed, he didn't fully understand the nature of his own secondary reactions. Neither he nor Gina recognized that his secondary emotional reactions—whether grumbling, withdrawal, cheerful deference, or anger— all served the same purpose, despite their diverse appearances.

Backstage, Brett was wrestling with his sense of worth. He had come to depend on Gina to provide that for him. When subtle changes took hold in their relationship, his confidence was shaken and his onstage performance became erratic.

Losing Focus

Brett and Gina's relationship took a turn for the worse when they started scrutinizing that erratic onstage performance. Both of them focused on his secondary emotional reactions—what was happening onstage rather than what was going on behind the scenes. And because Brett had trouble understanding his unpredictable secondary emotional responses, focusing on them made him feel all the more ineffective.

Unfortunately, we men are so determined to put on a good act that we make it difficult for women (and even ourselves) to focus on anything other than our secondary emotional reactions. This is a recipe for serious misunderstandings.

In chapter 7, I discussed one of the most common self-defeating sentiments women hold in regard to relationships: *If he loved me, he wouldn't act that way.* In Brett's case, his erratic behavior certainly appeared to be the product of waning love, but love wasn't the issue. Even though he still loved Gina and wished things were the way they used to be, his secondary emotional reactions were so distressing that Gina had trouble seeing past them. Despite his intentions, his behavior seemed tailor-made to trigger Gina's insecurity about being abandoned.

How to Help

No one can force another person to develop insight. Given the escalating nature of their conflict, Gina was certainly in no position to force insight upon Brett, nor was it her responsibility to do so. However, as a loving partner she was in a position to avoid getting drawn into the onstage drama. As half of the partnership, she could foster a climate in which it might be tolerable for Brett to drop his choreographed act and expose what was going on behind the scenes.

Shortly, I'll offer you eight tips on how to do just that. Consider them your backstage pass. There are no guarantees that your partner will let you see what's going on behind the scenes, but a good man will generally rise to the occasion, if you set a tone that enables him to do so. But before we get to that, I want to share some of the most common things women unintentionally do that keep their partner's true feelings hidden, leaving his secondary reactions to erode the health of the relationship.

Five Ways to Keep His Feelings Hidden

When Gina pressed Brett into explaining his actions, she wasn't trying to punish him, and she wasn't trying to make the problem worse. To the contrary, she was trying to rekindle the love they once felt for each other. But as you now know, the law of trying harder doesn't apply exclusively to men. Women can just as easily get locked into strategies that make a problem worse.

Here are a few ineffective problem-solving strategies that tend to lock men into unproductive patterns:

* Time traveling

* Not forgiving him

* Punishing him for talking

* Expecting him to read your mind

* Avoiding solutions

That might seem like a list of mistakes. On the other hand, you might think of them as problem-solving strategies that happen to function poorly. Personally, I find the latter to be more accurate and useful.

Time Traveling

I've discussed how men tend to focus more on the relationship problem at hand than on problems of the past or future. One of the more common frustrations I hear from men is that women tend to time travel during arguments, using a current argument as a springboard to discuss past mistakes or worries about the future.

I think there's a more balanced way to look at this. Women (or men, for that matter) who get drawn into the past during an argument often are trying to identify and eliminate problematic patterns. Similarly, going into the future (for example, by saying something like "How are you ever going to be able to stop spending so much time with your friends when we have kids?") can be an attempt to prevent current problems from repeating.

But that's not how it feels to men. To a man's mind, resurrecting past mistakes tells him that you haven't forgiven him and probably never will, and arguing about the future tells him that you don't trust him to solve problems or make improvements. Both of these messages are surefire ways to shut down communication. As one man put it: "We tend to close down when our girlfriends or wives want a serious conversation. That's because experience has taught us that the conversation can quickly escalate out of control. We end up being punished for everything we've ever done."

> ## How Men Think
>
> **"When men argue, we're arguing about the conflict at hand. Women seem to argue about what's at hand, plus past conflicts."**

Sometimes it's useful to bring up past events or future concerns. Sometimes they're entirely relevant to the current discussion. But before you do so during a disagreement with your partner, consider asking yourself whether it's necessary or helpful to bring up the past or future in that moment. Then, if you choose to do so, take the time to help your partner understand why the past or future is important to you. If he understands why it matters, he'll be less likely to feel cornered and hopeless.

Not Forgiving Him

Time traveling can give your partner the impression that you haven't forgiven him. But sometimes lack of forgiveness is more than an impression. In my clinical work with couples, women tend to be more prone to resurrecting past transgressions when feelings of injury or vulnerability arise. Sometimes men also have trouble letting go of the past, but by nature they tend to be more willing to forgive and forget. As I'll discuss in chapter 10, a different approach to forgiveness is part of men's social wiring.

Most of the women I've met who had difficulty forgiving are concerned about emotional safety. They worry that if they drop their guard or stop reminding their partner of the pain he caused, he will repeat his damaging mistakes. And sometimes, those concerns are well founded.

If your partner's transgressions or character are such that he doesn't deserve forgiveness—in other words, if it would be risky to forgive him and open yourself to further injury—the relationship is in need of serious repair, or it may be best to end it. But small transgressions are often better left in the past once the matter has been settled.

As discussed elsewhere, and as I'll explore in some depth in chapter 9, one of the most destructive things that can happen to a relationship is for the man to decide he can't win. Few things discourage men more quickly than a lack of forgiveness. Consider the sentiments of these two men:

* "What would cause me to lose respect for a woman? Retaliation for my past mistakes."

* "Women who won't forgive me for silly little mistakes get scratched right off my list. I've seen too many of my friends dragged down that path to a lifetime of misery."

Those brash words don't really capture the pain men experience when they believe they're powerless to bring happiness to the woman in their lives. In fact, those two quotes seem like wonderful examples of secondary emotional reactions: prideful withdrawal that serves to mask fear and vulnerability.

Another unfortunate outcome, perhaps worse than when a man exits a seemingly hopeless relationship, is when a man stays and comes to resent his partner for withholding forgiveness. Such a man will go to great lengths—anything from utter silence to substance abuse—to keep his emotions protected and hidden.

Punishing Him for Talking

Unquestionably, one of the most common complaints about men is their lack of communication. My survey was filled with comments like this from women: "I wish I understood why he retreats and clams up if I'm upset. That's when I need him the most. But he just hides, like he's riding out a hurricane. It makes me feel so alone and unloved."

Many women expressed a sort of desperation to connect with the men in their lives, as this statement reveals: "There's nothing more frustrating and painful than to feel a need to communicate with my partner about a problem (any kind of problem—not just about the relationship), and yet not feel welcome to approach him."

That frustration may be what leads many women to make the common mistake of punishing their partner when he finally opens up. I think punishment is rarely the intent, but certain types of responses can leave a man regretting his decision to share his feelings:

* "Why didn't you tell me this sooner?"

* "You shouldn't feel that way."

* "How can you think that?"

* "I'm hurt that you felt you couldn't tell me this before."

* "You thought what? Don't be silly."

Such things are often said with the intent of easing a partner's anxiety or fostering further communication, but they can leave a man feeling as if he made a mistake by opening up. If he already regards communication as risky, it won't take much to make him feel criticized. So even if you don't like the content of what your partner says, a wise response typically acknowledges his thoughts and feelings without criticizing how or when he spoke. Sometimes simply saying, "Thank you for telling me that," or giving your partner a hug will let him know that it's safe to open up to you.

Expecting Him to Read Your Mind

Earlier in the book, I discussed the different social styles of men and women. Women tend to prefer intimate, one-on-one connections, whereas men operate more comfortably in larger groups with looser connections. I believe that difference is at least partly to blame for one of the more common complaints from men. Here's how one man put it: "It's frustrating that we're supposed to know exactly what women are thinking and feeling, that we're supposed to read their minds."

This man is undoubtedly speaking of sentiments such as *If you cared, you'd know how I'm feeling* or *You should know why I'm angry*.

Generally, women operate more comfortably in intimately bonded relationships. That style of connection necessarily makes a person more skilled at anticipating the emotional states and needs of friends and loved ones.

In general, it makes sense to assume that other people work the same way you do. If you operate by anticipating others' needs, it's reasonable to assume that others work the same way. Therefore, you might assume that there's a problem if others don't anticipate your needs.

But men who operate more comfortably within looser, more numerous relationships may be speaking a different language than the women in their lives. Therefore, a failure to anticipate needs and emotional states may simply be the product of different social aptitudes that come with different skills.

A friend offered this example: "I had a load of laundry in the dryer, and my husband dumped it out on the floor when he did a load after mine. If I hated someone, maybe I would do that to them. He said since he thought the load was only dog blankets (it wasn't), it didn't matter that he dumped it on the floor." Initially, she was angry about what seemed like a lack of consideration. But as the two of them discussed it, they realized that they simply had different assumptions and different levels of subtlety in their communication. To her, dumping the laundry on the floor was tantamount to an insult. To him, it was just dog blankets and nothing more.

The bottom line? Expressing disappointment at a man's efforts, even if they're a bit misguided, is bound to make him feel ineffective (unless you can work it out, as my friend did). It's generally better to offer encouragement and help your partner understand what you'd prefer next time.

Avoiding Solutions

Here's another useful generalization: women often communicate to connect, whereas men generally communicate to solve problems. This is a common source of friction between the genders. Women can end up feeling invalidated when their problems aren't heard, and men can end up feeling frustrated when the problems aren't solved.

Here's what two women had to say about communication and problem solving:

* "We don't want men to fix everything for us. Sometimes we just want a warm, supportive response. It makes our problems seem more manageable when we know we have someone in our corner cheering for us."

* "Often women just want to complain, and we feel close to someone who listens without judgment. That person is forging a connection with us."

And here's what two men said about the same topic:

* "Some women don't like to fix problems. Instead, complaining about it is often enough. This, of course, just means that the problem comes back later and we go through the cycle all over again."

* "Why is the act of complaining enough to calm women down? I find it frustrating when I complain and then realize that I haven't accomplished anything to fix the problem."

It seems like an irreconcilable difference between the genders, but it needn't be. These things are negotiable. Just as a woman should feel free to tell a man that she wants his compassion rather than his solutions, a man should feel free to speak up when the lack of a solution is a source of anxiety or frustration for him.

A lot of men don't realize that it's okay to talk about how we talk to each other. There's even a word for it: metacommunication. Good metacommunication allows couples to make room for different styles.

If you're someone for whom venting about problems is enough and the relationship consists mainly of your venting, you may be shortchanging your partner if he wants to help you solve problems. In fact, one of the reasons some men are hesitant to listen to women complain is that they fear the discussion will continue indefinitely, the problems will never be solved, and they'll be doomed to a lifetime of impotent listening. They fear they'll never experience the satisfaction of helping the most important person in their lives.

Eight Steps to Your Backstage Pass

Now that we've examined the kind of tactics that can keep a man's emotions hidden behind the scenes, let's look at more productive strategies. You can't force a man to express himself, but you can foster an encouraging environment.

For a good man to show you what's going on behind the scenes, he must trust you. Most men are quite skittish about exposing their inner workings. Trust can't be requested or demanded. Like building a savings account, building trust takes time. The following tips will help you create an environment in which your partner feels safe enough to expose his feelings and confide in you:

* Let him please you.

* Give brownie points.

* Embrace simplicity.

* Be specific when you express your needs.

* Weigh his actions as much as his words.

* Have fun.

* Understand his silence.

* Be intimate.

Let Him Please You

If your partner wants to make you happy, resist the urge to argue against compliments or reject gifts. It doesn't matter if you just started dating, or you've been married for twenty-five years. Be gracious when he fixes something, acknowledge him when he tries to please you, and throw him a bone once in a while by taking his advice when his advice is good. A good man wants to be the most important thing in the world to the woman in his life. You have the power to give him that gift—at least sometimes.

Give Brownie Points

Because men are geared toward large social groups, we're accustomed to using social currency. We track intangible exchanges of favors, acts of kindness, personal slights, and debts.

Think back to the last time you heard someone say, "I'm going to call in some favors." I'm betting it was a man who uttered those words. Social currency is a reflection of men's social style. Because we worry about our standing in the group, we keep ledgers in our heads.

Even in intimate relationships, we tend to keep track of the favors we perform. If we think our partners aren't noticing, it's like discovering deposits never found their way into our bank account and the balance is zero.

You can use our social style to your advantage. Give brownie points in whatever form your partner would appreciate. Simple acknowledgment is sufficient for most guys. If you choose to return favors in a way that would be meaningful to him, I'm sure he won't protest.

Don't worry that you need to keep the same sort of social ledger that men do. A good man typically won't try to "call in favors" from the woman he loves. He doesn't apply the same quid pro quo thinking to his partner that he does to men. He just wants to know that you're aware of how much he does for you.

Embrace Simplicity

The complexity and openness of women's emotions is one of the things men find attractive about them. In fact, that admiration was one of the more common themes in my survey. But expressing emotion can be exhausting for men. Even though our emotions run as deeply as yours, we're accustomed to blunting them and keeping them under wraps, and we often prefer to keep our focus outward rather than inward. As a result, when we express a thought or feeling, it has often been boiled down to its essence. Sometimes this leaves women searching for more details or deeper meaning, which can be frustrating for men. Here's what some of the men in my survey had to say on this topic:

* "I wish women understood that men are basically simple creatures. We say what we think. There's no reason to make things more complicated than necessary."

* "When you ask me what I'm thinking and I say 'nothing,' I really wasn't thinking about anything. I don't really think about you when I'm busy at work or away, but that doesn't mean I don't love you. My brain just does one thing at a time. (I would love to see a transcript of a woman's thoughts for an hour. I bet it would be like a hurricane.)"

* "You'd be hard-pressed to find a man who isn't satisfied with the basics, like a dog. All we want is something to eat, somewhere to rest, someone to love us, and someone to pet us at the end of the day and assure us that this one has gone well and they'd like us around for another."

Though it may be tempting to search for the deeper meaning behind a man's words, sometimes there isn't much to uncover. If you take us at our word when we tell you how we feel, we're more likely to trust you when there's more complex behind-the-scenes business to discuss.

Be Specific When You Express Your Needs

We men function better when we know exactly what you want from us. Don't take it personally if we don't anticipate your needs accurately. Here's what one man said about this: "What frustrates me most is how women don't communicate specifically what they want or need. They unintentionally force men to guess at what they're trying to convey, and of course we're in trouble when we guess wrong. They accuse us of not paying attention when we're trying to get it right!"

When we miss the target, give us points for trying and set us on the right path. That will help us be more effective next time, and it will keep us from feeling hopeless.

Weigh His Actions as Much as His Words

Men often rely more on actions than on words to convey meaning. As one man explained, "Because men relate by doing things together, we rely more on nonverbal communication."

When we're talking to you, the women in our lives, we may rely on actions more than words, and admittedly that makes you work harder. One woman explained how she began translating her man's actions: "I think I've finally learned to watch men's actions for guidance on how they truly feel. Sometimes I even have to say back to myself what I think his actions mean: He did X, which I believe is him saying he feels Y."

Listening to a man's actions doesn't involve a decoder ring; it just takes willingness to notice the meanings behind deeds. Men want to be heard as much as women, even if we sometimes communicate differently.

Admittedly, there is some irony in this. On one hand, we ask you to avoid reading too much meaning into our words (or lack thereof). On the other, we expect you to understand the meanings behind our actions. However, there is consistency within this seeming double standard: when words fail us, watch our behavior.

Have Fun

Your happiness is one of the first things we look for when we judge our effectiveness in a relationship. If you're happy, we figure we're performing adequately. Here's what a couple of guys had to say about this:

* "A woman who laughs at my jokes makes me feel good inside."

* "Our best moments are playing, joking, and just talking and connecting after a hard day."

* "One woman I know gets it. She told me that after thirty years of marriage, she knows how to make her husband happy: 'Every so often I cook him a steak and take him up to bed.' Yes, we really are that simple."

Unless you intend to send the impression that we're performing poorly, have fun with us. Even though we become more serious-minded as the relationship matures, we still want to enjoy our time with you.

Understand His Silence

It's easy to interpret silence as a form of punishment or cruelty, and sometimes it is. But silence can have different meanings. Here are a few more thoughts from men on their silence:

* "Being quiet is a way to process, much in the same way that women need to talk to process."

* "When I go silent, it's because I just don't want to get hurt anymore. I want the argument to end, and I want to protect myself."

* "When we're quiet, it doesn't mean we're unhappy. Sometimes we just need to regroup and recover in our own way. Basically, sharing isn't always the best way for us to heal."

The question is, what does silence mean for the man in your life? If he uses silence to solve problems, as many men do, then you might heed this man's advice: "Give me some space when I retreat. I would rather process whatever is bothering me than be impulsive and regret not thinking it through."

Be Intimate

I know how it is. You're tired. You don't feel attractive. Maybe you don't feel like being intimate because your partner hasn't been acting the way you want him to lately. But here's the thing about intimacy, or just about any other activity: when you start your body down the path, your heart and mind typically follow. This is true for men and women alike.

It's tempting here to insert all manner of qualifications about intimacy, but I'll only mention a few. I'm not suggesting that any woman should have sex with a man if she doesn't want to. Nor should she be intimate with him if there are physical or emotional problems, or if the man isn't committed. (If he's equivocating, he isn't committed yet.) You know whether or not you love him. Perhaps we can leave it at that.

Helping Your Partner Communicate

This talk about what you can do for your partner may leave you with the impression that I think his communication is your responsibility. It isn't. He's the one who must decide whether he's going to let you see what goes on behind the scenes.

Opening up is a genuinely daunting task for many men because we've been well taught to keep our thoughts and feelings hidden, even from ourselves. Expressing emotion can make us feel as if we're breaking rules that have kept us safe.

But even though expressing ourselves is difficult, it's our responsibility, not yours. All I'm suggesting is that you try to make it easier for him—and maybe have some fun along the way. If he chooses to remain emotionally untouchable, at least you'll know that you've done your best to foster a welcoming environment.

For the Man in Your Life:
How to Prevent Arguments from Getting Out of Control

Guys, you know that feeling you get when the woman in your life is upset with you? That gut-wrenching anxiety? The tension that gnaws at you? You just want that feeling to go away, right? Well guess what: so does she.

Unfortunately, many couples stay stuck with those feelings because their problem-solving styles are different, even though both partners want peace. For example, men often retreat from an argument and go silent. Why? Because they want that feeling to go away. Many women, on the other hand, will pursue their partner and try to engage him in conversation. Why? For the same reason. She wants that feeling to go away.

Those are incompatible strategies aimed at the same result: a peaceful relationship. Creating that peace usually involves a bit of talking and communication. The problem is, most of us men have been taught to keep our feelings under wraps, so it takes more time for us to gather our thoughts, and women get frustrated.

If that's the case for you, one of the most useful things you can do is educate your partner about your silence. Explain why you stop talking. Let her know that it isn't personal and that taking some time to reflect on problems helps you solve them. If you want your partner to respect your problem-solving style, you're going to have to meet her halfway by explaining it to her and making some compromises.

Most of us men just want our partners to be happy. In the words of one woman who shared her thoughts with me, "Reassurance and a few words go a lot further than being quiet and thinking you're doing the right thing."

Chapter 9

Relationship Quicksand

M en are well trained at partitioning their lives and maintaining walls between work, marriage, social activities, and so on. I believe that men also have a unique ability to wall off a certain flavor of depression that shows up mainly in their relationships. They can function well in their professional and social lives and be utterly depressed at home.

A common symptom of depression is decreased activity. People struggling with depression often limit themselves to a few safe places, and no longer enjoy or participate in things that used to bring happiness.

I've met many men whose home lives have become severely constrained. At work and with buddies, they're the same old guy. But with their partner, they're withdrawn and lethargic and seem to have the demeanor of a dog who has been beaten down and is simply trying to avoid the next assault. They've given up any hope of enjoying their relationship or bringing joy to their partner.

These men have stopped trying. They disengage entirely from conflict with their partner because, in their experience, they can't win. They stop trying to please her because they think they'll never succeed, and they no longer behave lovingly because they've lost their sense of effectiveness. They've left the relationship in spirit, if not in body.

This is relationship quicksand because the more a woman tries to rescue the relationship using well-intentioned problem-solving approaches that have become part of a destructive pattern, the deeper the relationship sinks. The struggle to fix the relationship becomes part of the problem, as we'll see in the next case study.

One note before you read on: Even if your relationship is healthy, the tips in this chapter build on those in chapter 8 and can help you foster an environment in which your partner is more willing to communicate. Again, you can't make him talk, but you can make doing so easier for him at no cost to yourself.

• Nancy and Eric

Nancy and Eric had a small wedding since it was the second marriage for each of them. Nancy's first husband was a quiet, pensive accountant. The two of them had grown apart after a few years, and Nancy became increasingly frustrated with his apparent inability to speak his mind. She felt that he had a habit of withholding his desires and then playing the wounded martyr.

Eric's first wife was similarly passive. He was routinely frustrated at her unwillingness or inability to state her wishes. Eventually, she expressed irreparable dissatisfaction with the relationship and asked for a divorce.

When Eric met Nancy, she was like a breath of fresh air. She was outspoken, expressive, and opinionated in a way that was wonderfully refreshing to Eric. Never again would he have to guess at his partner's desires. He felt confident that this relationship wouldn't end because his partner refused to express herself.

Eric had been raised to be a peacekeeper and a caretaker. His parents taught him to be attentive to those around him, and he enjoyed the role. Whenever Nancy expressed a desire, Eric was happy to oblige.

Time passed, and Nancy and Eric evolved into increasingly polarized roles in their relationship. This isn't unusual; people often become more pronounced versions of themselves as relationships mature.

Nancy's outspokenness evolved into a tendency to be demanding. She found herself issuing directives to Eric almost as if she were his supervisor, and a micromanaging one at that. If he failed to perform a task to her satisfaction, she criticized him openly and sometimes aggressively. However, she didn't enjoy that role. She was simply filling the void created by Eric's hesitance to express *his* wishes. She wanted a more assertive husband, and she actually appreciated the rare occasions when Eric stood up for himself.

As Eric became increasingly anxious about being scolded by Nancy, she began to feel as if, unwittingly, she'd been put in charge of the relationship. She sensed shades of her first husband in Eric, and she wished he would assume some of the power and responsibility in the relationship.

Meanwhile, Eric was becoming resentful. *She's never happy,* he thought. *How did I hitch myself to such a nagging harpy?* His resentment turned into resistance, and he found himself avoiding Nancy, ignoring her demands and, uncharacteristically, performing half measures. If she asked him to wash her car, he gave it a quick once-over rather than the thorough cleaning he used to take pride in.

Nancy sensed Eric retreating and the relationship faltering. In times of stress, people naturally turn to strategies that have worked in the past. In Nancy's case, that meant taking charge. She became even more directive with Eric, and her uncertainty about his feelings for her caused her to notice every imperfection in his performance and character. As a result, she became more demanding than ever.

Of course, that just strengthened the destructive pattern they had fallen into, and Eric's response didn't help. The other side of his admirable peacekeeping nature was the difficulty he experienced in expressing his needs. He tried to avoid Nancy's criticism, but his usual passivity no longer kept her at bay.

Out of a desperate desire to escape the anxiety and resentment caused by Nancy's escalating criticism, he began to take refuge in alcohol. Knowing Nancy would disapprove, he kept his drinking a secret, hiding bottles in his car and in the garage.

Alcohol also served to insulate him from the nagging and miserable thought that he was once again failing at marriage. He didn't know how to fix the marriage, but he didn't want to endure a second divorce. He felt stuck. While he was the same old gregarious Eric at work and with friends, at home he was a shell of a man. He had given up.

Most nights Nancy found Eric asleep in front of the TV, drunk. She felt utterly alone. He wouldn't even argue with her. She felt like she was living with a ghost.

How to Prevent or Escape Relationship Quicksand

Nancy and Eric's relationship isn't a pretty picture. She feels abandoned and shortchanged. She's wondering how the upbeat, accommodating man she married transformed into a depressed alcoholic. And although she has trouble expressing it, she's heartbroken that the man she loves has become so unhappy, beaten down, and numb. They're stuck in relationship quicksand. He's no longer responding to any attempt to repair the relationship. Even good men give up sometimes.

Relationship quicksand can stem from a number of problems. I've seen it happen in cases like Eric's, where a power imbalance leaves a man feeling impotent in the struggle to achieve happiness or be effective in a relationship. Sometimes a woman's untreated mood disorder, substance use, or other difficulties leave her partner feeling hopeless about pleasing her. It also happens when a woman withholds intimacy and her partner fears he's doomed to a sexless existence. And it definitely can happen when nagging and disrespect leave a man thinking, *There's no way to please her, so why bother trying?*

Relationship quicksand can be particularly insidious because we men are so skilled at compartmentalizing our lives. A man like Eric can be utterly miserable at home and still perform adequately elsewhere, hiding his problem from friends and family. If he feels trapped in his relationship for financial or emotional reasons, he may stick around but remain disengaged for years or even a lifetime.

When, for whatever reason, a man has decided that it's hopeless to continue putting effort into a relationship, the relationship is in significant danger. Luckily, few relationships are beyond repair if both parties are willing to make an honest effort in healing the rift. However, it's unlikely that couples in a situation as bad as Nancy and Eric's will be able to rekindle their love without outside help. I'll discuss what to look for in a therapist toward the end of this chapter, but first I'd like to offer some strategies for escaping or, better yet, preventing relationship quicksand:

* If there's a problem, name it.

* Be someone your partner wants to be around.

* Respond to primary emotional reactions.

* Create a pattern escape hatch.

* Accept peace offerings.

* Don't assume he understands.

* Rebuild intimacy.

* Seek couples therapy.

If There's a Problem, Name It

Nancy and Eric's struggle was exacerbated by their difficulties in speaking openly about their problems. Neither had had much training in communication from family or previous relationships, and both were saddled with powerful impulses to handle the problem without words—Nancy by taking charge, and Eric by being the peacemaker.

As mentioned, many men communicate more by way of actions than with words. But that doesn't mean we don't want to attach at least a few words to a problem. Perhaps because we're so driven to find solutions, we function better when we know the name of the problem, be it a fouled spark plug or malfunctioning relationship pattern. We want to know what we're trying to fix.

When it comes to labeling problems, specific is good. Here are a few ways that Nancy and Eric might have begun to label their pattern. Notice that none of them are critical or blaming. They are simply factual descriptions of the pattern, not the people:

* *I notice that each of us is working really hard to get what we need from the other.*

* *Does it seem like we've stopped trying to please each other?*

* *Does it seem to you that I've been making almost all of the decisions lately?*

Attaching clear, specific labels to problematic patterns—even if the labels are imperfect—helps men in several ways. First, the mere act of attaching a few words to a problem creates a bit of distance from it. When one person can say, "Hey, I think we're doing it again," both suddenly become more aware of the behavior and less attached to it. It loses some of its power over them. (You probably noticed that a couple of those examples were phrased as questions. Nonaccusatory questions are a nice way to introduce a label while giving your partner the opportunity to agree or to offer a different idea.)

Second, naming the problem gives men something to sink their teeth into. It gives us a focal point for that introspective, mechanistic problem-solving style discussed earlier.

Third, when a couple can agree on the name and the nature of the problem they're facing, they suddenly have a common goal, even if it's tenuous at first. We men like to team up with other people to do constructive things. We're more likely to open up and work toward a solution when we know our partner is on our side and focused on the same goal.

Attaching a name to a problematic pattern may seem like a small step, but it's an important one.

Be Someone He Wants to Be Around

The arguments and destructive patterns that couples fall into often involve a sense of lost intimacy and connection. All of us, men and women alike, naturally feel anxious and upset when the person we love seems to be slipping away from us. We want the same love and respect we once had.

It's also natural to feel wounded when love seems to be slipping away, but it may cause us to turn to strategies meant to restore the relationship, but which ultimately push our partner even further away. The man who retreats in a stereotypical fashion, the woman who pursues or nags, the partner who tries to create jealousy, the partner who punishes with the cold shoulder or barbed comments—all are actually seeking a way to restore the relationship. They want to feel safe once again.

But these natural responses transform us in ways that are painfully ironic. Once upon a time, we were people our partners couldn't wait to be with. They thought about us when they were at work, they sent us romantic emails just to let us know they were thinking about us, and we were the ones they turned to with their problems.

Relationship problems—or more accurately, the way we respond to them—can turn us into people our partners try to avoid. I believe this is a particular challenge for women because men are more prone to withdrawing from relationships, placing women in a disadvantageous position.

This is an example of the demand-withdrawal pattern discussed in chapter 7. When one person withdraws, it unfairly places the other in the position of being the pursuer, perhaps resorting to nagging and complaining. This is a dangerous path because the pursuing partner increasingly becomes the "troublemaker"—the person who will never be pleased. The more one person withdraws—and this person is usually the man—the more the other pursues, makes demands, and seems unreasonable.

This is when manners and consideration can begin to slip. When kindness recedes from a relationship, disrespect and resentment take its place. This is poisonous to relationships.

The Importance of Respect

As challenging as it can be, difficult times are precisely when it's most important to be the person our partners fell in love with. Especially when discussing difficult topics, we need to demonstrate that we still think our partners are worthy of respect. And let's be honest, sometimes we have to fake it.

It's undoubtedly difficult to be polite with a man who withdraws from the relationship. But rather than allowing frustration to win out, try the first tip in this section and name the problem: "I notice that I'm feeling compelled to chase you down and force you to talk to me."

It's also important to respect your partner—and yourself—enough to let him handle whatever portion of the problem lies on his end. When a woman harasses a man into conversing, she effectively relieves him of his responsibility to manage whatever difficulties he's facing. When he combats her about talking, he's distracted from the question of why he isn't talking.

Here's an example of how a woman might express that she respects her partner enough to let him manage his own problems while also respecting her boundaries: "I'm going to try to resist the urge to corner you into conversations. I don't like the way it makes either of us feel. You know that I'd like to talk. I'm relying on you to help us through this."

At that point, the pursuer is freed of her misplaced duty to protect her partner. She's free to be the person she wants to be, and to be the person her partner fell in love with. Now it's *his* problem to solve. (However, he may not know how to begin solving it—a problem I'll address shortly.)

The Risks of Respect

Allowing your partner to address his own problem can be difficult and scary. What if he's unwilling to converse after that point? What would it say about the relationship? I suspect that this variety of fear keeps many couples trapped in a demand-withdrawal pattern. As long as they remain in that pattern, they forestall the possibility of revealing something unpleasant about the relationship, such as the possibility that the man has no interest in maintaining it.

However, there's a more likely and less threatening possibility. Many men honestly don't know how to converse at the level women often desire, for a number of reasons. Maybe they've never been exposed to that level of conversation. Maybe they tried it but felt punished for doing so. Maybe they're painfully averse to being emotionally vulnerable. If this is the root of the problem, it might help your partner if you remind him that he has options. Rather than diving right into a difficult conversation with you, he might talk to a friend first, see a therapist alone, go to couples counseling with you, confide in a relative, and so on.

Take it from someone who has been there: some men honestly don't know how to approach these things. If that's the case, it won't help your partner, nor will it further your cause, to lose respect for him. Offering a bit of guidance when he needs it, respecting him enough to let him struggle with his own difficulties, and being the person he fell in love with—these things are harder to do, but ultimately they're more rewarding for everyone.

Respond to Primary Emotional Reactions

Men's secondary emotional reactions can be so well practiced that they don't even recognize them. That's not new information, but you may be surprised to learn that many men admire the emotional skills that women possess, as these men amply convey:

* "I love the way women don't fear emotion. I love the way they live with open hearts. It makes them more vulnerable to feeling sad, but I think it also opens them up to feel a level of contentment and joy beyond what men can experience."

* "Women can be very kind and aware of the needs of others in a way that would never occur to me."

Clearly, it isn't women's responsibility to make men understand themselves. But you can help us, if you wish, by responding to our primary emotional reactions rather than our secondary reactions.

For example, Eric's secondary reaction to Nancy's demands was an extreme form of withdrawal. His *primary* reaction was a feeling of frustration and hopelessness. Although Nancy wasn't especially well practiced in negotiating these kinds of difficulties, she didn't need be an expert to help Eric through it. Had she acknowledged to herself that something was going on behind the scenes, she could have approached Eric with simple curiosity about it.

She could have begun by putting a name to the problem and then simply expressing openness about it, even if she didn't understand exactly what was happening, perhaps saying something like "It seems like you're shutting down, but I'm pretty sure that's not what you want from our marriage. Can we try to figure out what's going on?" A good man like Eric would probably have felt relieved by this softer approach.

Create a Pattern Escape Hatch

In chapter 7, I discussed destructive patterns and the importance of replacing them. Creating an escape hatch is one way to interrupt a destructive pattern. It can also reassure your partner that you're searching for a solution to the problem rather than blaming him.

Once you and your partner have put words to the problem and started down the path of identifying secondary emotional reactions, you can begin using a safe word to interrupt the pattern as it's beginning to repeat—and before the damage is done.

Here's how it works: The two of you agree that you'll take a break at *the first sign* that a destructive pattern is resurfacing and you're about to have the same old argument again. (Recall the dashboard warning lights discussed in chapter 7.) Some couples agree to a whimsical safe word, like "Sasquatch" or "jambalaya." Others agree to simply say something more direct, like "Let's take a break." Once you learn to successfully interrupt the pattern, you'll both be in a good position to return to the discussion and replace the problematic behavior using the process outlined in the section "As Challenging as 1-2-3," in chapter 7.

There are a couple of important steps in creating an escape hatch. First, you must negotiate the terms. Agree on the word or phrase that you'll use and the length of time you'll wait before returning to the conversation.

Second, give yourselves permission to make mistakes. Using the escape hatch can be a difficult skill to master. One or both partners may have trouble disengaging during an argument or difficulty returning to the conversation after the agreed-upon time has elapsed. In fact, it's common to avoid returning to the conversation because of anxiety about how the conversation will go. It's also common to feel that the other person is invoking the escape hatch to win or escape an argument. Missteps are normal. Renegotiate the rules if necessary, and try again the next time a destructive pattern emerges. When handled with good faith and good intentions, even mistakes can turn out to be healing experiences.

I've noticed that, in general, men are more comfortable with the escape hatch than women are. Men often seem more willing to break away from damaging conversations. Perhaps that's because men who are teetering toward relationship quicksand feel as if there's no way for them to escape a repetitive conflict. The escape hatch can create hope for these men, and building the escape hatch together can help rebuild trust.

Accept Peace Offerings

I knew a man who, after the first session of couples therapy, changed the oil in his wife's car. She was accustomed to taking her car to the local lube shop a couple of times a year, but on this occasion he decided to do it himself and save her the trip. You can probably guess where this story is going: it was more than just an oil change.

The man found their first session helpful. In particular, he appreciated that his wife openly took responsibility for her portion of their communication problems. That gave him hope. The oil change was an offering of gratitude.

His wife, being smart and insightful, recognized the offering for what it was. She didn't complain that she would have preferred a romantic dinner. She was wise enough to know the romantic dinner would come soon enough—once her husband felt he could lower his defenses enough to engage with her more romantically.

She accepted the peace offering, acknowledged it, and expressed gratitude. That small act on her part encouraged her husband to continue his efforts at rebuilding. An unkind, critical, or indifferent response, on the other hand, would have discouraged him.

Male communication can be subtle. We aren't the socially inept creatures that TV sitcoms portray us to be. We're versed in the language of large, loosely connected groups where social capital is the coin of the realm and subtle gestures often carry significant meaning.

Don't Assume He Understands

Just as women can miss the subtext of male communication, men can miss the intent behind women's subtler signals. This happened to a couple I knew. He couldn't seem to understand that when his wife asked him to walk the dog with her, she was really looking for some time alone with him. She had heard that men relate to others better when they're engaged in an activity together, so she was trying to speak his language.

He missed the point. He assumed she simply wanted someone to pick up after the dog or to take over when the dog started tugging on its leash. He walked with her without complaining, but privately he was mildly annoyed at his wife's new habit of interrupting his busy schedule for something so trivial.

Fortunately, they were able to sort out the situation after he grumbled about it one evening. He admitted that he had been feeling annoyed that she thrust a new responsibility on him without discussing it, and she clarified that she was trying to connect with him in a way that might be meaningful to him. Once he understood her intention, he appreciated her effort, and they continued to take walks together.

Don't assume that we understand what you're really trying to say to us, and don't make us guess. We want to please you, but we're bound to guess wrong at least part of the time. That leaves you feeling disappointed and us feeling defeated.

Rebuild Intimacy

I'll forgo euphemism here. Men like sex. Most men will tell you that they *need* sex. That may seem overstated, but there is a grain of truth to it.

One review of the scientific literature on this topic found that frequent intimacy improves mood, immune functioning, and cardiovascular health and has other direct health benefits (Brody 2010), with most of the benefits applying to both men and women. (Interestingly, that study suggested that some forms of sexual activity can have reverse effects. For example, replacing sex with frequent masturbation can actually lower a man's mood.) Among men who engage in sex frequently, rates of prostate cancer are lower, and the same is true for women and rates of breast cancer. The study even found that men who have more sex and women who enjoy it more live longer.

The benefits aren't just physical. Frequent sex has such a profound effect on perceptions of intimacy that it can even buffer the anxiety of people who struggle with insecure attachment styles (Little, McNulty, and Russel 2010). These people, who may have experienced neglectful parenting that makes it difficult for them to feel secure in adult relationships, manage their anxieties more successfully when they have frequent intimate relations with a loving partner.

Sex, as long as it's caring and enjoyable, benefits both women and men. Of course, men have a reputation for having a larger sexual appetite. Middle-aged men, in particular, express the desire for more frequent sex (Smith et al. 2011). That may be because the demands of middle-aged life (parenting, working, and so on) interfere with intimacy.

My point is that for men, sexual intimacy promotes well-being, and it often helps us feel closer to our partners. But when a couple is in relationship quicksand, there's a good chance that sexual intimacy has dropped off. In any case where there's a shred of hope for rekindling the relationship, I believe it's a mistake to forgo physical relations (barring physical problems, emotional difficulties, or health concerns, of course). Forgoing sex eliminates one of the most important ways a woman can foster closeness with her partner. Yet I've met many women who crave emotional closeness with their partner but have effectively cut him off. It's difficult to capture in words how discouraging this is to men.

Withholding sex can drive men out of relationships. When men feel they're being denied intimacy, intimacy becomes their focus. Many men will begin looking elsewhere for emotional and physical connection when they can't find it at home.

I realize that this is a hot-button topic, and that sex and trust are tightly linked for most women. I would never suggest that anyone put themselves in an intimate and vulnerable position with someone they feel they can't trust. Nor am I suggesting that women "put out" to save a relationship.

At the same time, any relationship worth saving should be well-rounded and mutually satisfying. Research shows that physical intimacy—or lack of it—has a profound effect on men. Here's how one man put it: "Sex is one way men understand and express their love. Of course, there are men who want sex only for the pleasure. But I'm willing to wager that a majority of men are looking for sex with a strong sense of emotional connection. There are few greater joys than the loving acceptance a woman gives a man through sex."

Rekindling intimacy in a struggling relationship can be a challenge for both partners. Sometimes a little guidance is required. That brings me to my final tip for handling relationship quicksand.

Seek Couples Therapy

Someone once told me that good advice is one of the most valuable things a person can buy. When couples therapy is done well, it's a small investment that can prevent a lifetime of struggle and unhappiness.

Unfortunately, many men are intimidated by couples therapy. And who can blame them? My profession is quite female-friendly, sometimes to the point of being unfriendly toward men. With that as background, here are a few tips on how to persuade a hesitant man that it's time to seek some valuable outside advice.

First, bear in mind that couples therapy may be quite threatening to your partner. It may go against all of his training in keeping his emotions hidden safely behind the scenes. Make sure he knows that you won't let the therapist team up with you to paint him as the bad guy. Many men fear that will happen. Assure him also that you won't stand for any antimale bias from the therapist (and don't assume that a male therapist won't take an antimale stance). Also assure your partner that you'll take your share of responsibility.

Make sure your partner gets to participate in choosing the therapist, and promise that you won't make a second appointment until the two of you have discussed it privately. Look for a highly trained professional with plenty of experience and a good sense of humor. Humor helps most men relax and engage in therapy. And don't be afraid to shop around. These days, many therapists offer a free initial consultation.

Some of the things I suggested in this chapter, like naming the problem and responding to primary emotional reactions, sound easy on paper but can be quite difficult to do in real life. A good therapist can help a couple stay focused and avoid falling back into old patterns. In my male, problem-solving estimation, it's better to seek assistance than to struggle indefinitely.

What About Nancy and Eric?

Therapy would be an excellent idea for a couple like Nancy and Eric, especially because they both entered the marriage with a troubling relationship history and communication deficits. A good therapist could help them identify and prioritize the important issues, such as Eric's withdrawal and substance abuse, the extreme power imbalance in the relationship, and the unproductive ways in which Nancy expresses her needs. That's a trifecta of destructive patterns, each of which can be quite difficult to overcome, making professional help all the more important.

Despite their serious difficulties, couples like Nancy and Eric can rebuild satisfying, close relationships. In their case in particular, I'd hope that the therapist would help bring Eric's strengths back into the relationship.

For the Man in Your Life:
Emasculation Isn't Good for Anyone

Guys, this chapter was about men who have given up on their relationship. They feel beaten down, and they are no longer the men they want to be.

I'm sure you've seen it: a man who hides out in his garage, his office, or the bar because he's lost all hope for a good relationship with his wife or girlfriend. He can't stand being with her, but he stays in the relationship to avoid emotional or financial repercussions.

That guy has essentially emasculated himself. He's depressed. He's no longer a fully functioning man in a mutually beneficial relationship. He has given up and taken the path of least resistance.

If you are that guy—if you're hiding from your wife or girlfriend while life passes by—get help. Don't struggle alone. Find a friend, a mentor, or a therapist who can help you once again be the man you want to be—and a man your partner wants to be around.

You don't have to fix it in one day. In fact, it might take a while. Just start by putting words to the problem. Initiate a conversation about it with someone. It's the right thing to do—and the manly thing to do.

Chapter 10

Good Things That Good Men Bring to Relationships

W e all know that men love TV. (I keep a picture of mine in my wallet!) However, TV doesn't always love men. I'm sure you've seen sitcoms in which only women possess relationship wisdom, and these long-suffering heroines must routinely rescue their hapless men from pitiable male ineptitude. That's good for a laugh, but relationships work best when there's room for two skill sets. In fact, some anthropologists believe that the failure to incorporate both male and female traits into their culture and relationships is one of the primary reasons Neanderthals perished (Kuhn and Stiner 2006).

Our distant ancestors, on the other hand, learned to capitalize on both female and male strengths. They divided their responsibilities accordingly, and that gave our species a profound survival advantage (Kuhn and Stiner 2006). Of course, a lot has changed over the millennia. We now have televisions, for one thing. But this remains constant: the healthiest relationships have room for both female and male strengths.

What Makes Good Men Good at Relationships

Would you guess that a little boy's willingness to jump his bicycle off a makeshift ramp would make him better at relationships in the future? What about his willingness to face the offensive line of his peewee football team's unbeaten rival or the expectation that he not cry if he gets hurt during the game? Would you ever imagine that his coach requiring him to shake hands with the opposing team, regardless of the outcome of the game, could make him a great husband or boyfriend?

It's true. Experiences like those contribute to a boy's ability to become a good and skillful mate someday far in the future. How? To get a glimpse, let's take a look at how girls and boys handle empathy.

Girls up to their early teens have better developed empathy for other children who are suffering than boys do, and they're better able to understand the sources of pain, whether their own pain or that of others (Garaigordobil 2009). For example, a girl would be more likely to intuitively understand that a friend is sad because she was excluded from a group.

Boys are obviously capable of understanding sources of pain, but their focus is elsewhere. Whether we chalk the difference up to nature, nurture, or nature amplified by nurture (my preference), boys are generally more focused on being tough, walking it off, reducing vulnerability, and getting themselves or their teammates back in the literal or figurative game. Boys don't dwell much on sources of pain. They aren't unconcerned with emotion, but they are more concerned with outcome.

This difference in empathy and pain analysis is well documented, and in my experience it's routinely presented as a deficit on the part of boys. That judgment seems unnecessary and shortsighted. Empathy is valuable, but stoicism is equally valuable depending on the context. The beautiful part is that we don't have to settle for one or the other. We can have both. In fact, we need both.

Suppose a group of people were lost in the wilderness and had to find their way home. Empathy would be an important skill because it would help the group cohere. But equally important would be the ability to see beyond sources of pain and focus on getting home.

Couples and families routinely face ongoing stressful situations. We may not get lost in the woods often, but we are confronted with financial difficulties, health problems, and any number of other challenges. The sublime beauty of blending male and female traits is the ability to bring the best of both worlds to any problem. To continue the lost-in-the-woods scenario, empathy ensures that sources of pain are identified and attended to. Stoicism, on the other hand, ensures that we recover quickly, reduce our vulnerability, and keep moving toward safety. Both are necessary, and that may be the perfect example of one of the reasons Neanderthals perished while our ancestors flourished.

The empathy-stoicism dichotomy is just one example of complementary traits. In this chapter, I'll explore several valuable male traits that complement female strengths, based in part on what women told me they like most about having men in their lives. But first, let me revisit my disclaimer about generalizations. There really are no male or female traits; there are simply traits that one gender, on average, possesses in greater quantity or uses differently. Personally, I find it both odd and wonderful that women tend to make up for whatever qualities men lack, and vice versa.

Men and women can complement each other in a relationship like yin and yang, heaven and earth, or beer and pretzels. Any male-female team that overlooks half of its emotional and cognitive assets is like an engine with half its spark plugs missing. Sure, it can limp along, but why not fire on all cylinders? Here, then, are some of the most valuable, and often overlooked, qualities that men can bring to relationships:

* Emotional protection

* Forgiving and forgetting

* The joy of simplicity

* Useful stoicism

* Goal orientation

* Playfulness

Emotional Protection

Men have historically been protectors. Women certainly aren't helpless, especially in our modern age, but the protective skills men have developed over thousands of generations are still available to any woman who wishes to capitalize on them.

Take Pete and Amy, a couple struggling to manage a group of rental properties they purchased together. As the realities of being landlords set in (midnight plumbing repairs, tax assessments, insurance costs, and so on), Pete and Amy increasingly fretted and disagreed over the properties. The issues with their rental properties invaded their family dinners, their weekends, and even their sex life.

Through couples therapy, they realized that Amy didn't really want to be involved in day-to-day property management. When they purchased the properties, they had assumed that partnership meant they had to equally share the anxiety and decision making, but Amy reluctantly admitted that she wanted Pete to take the lead. She had kept that to herself for fear of burdening him with the decision making that she found to be so unpleasant.

Amy was surprised to learn that Pete was happy to oblige. In fact, relieving her of the stress made him feel good, and he was thrilled to eliminate the source of so many arguments between them. They negotiated a new arrangement in which Pete managed the properties on his own except for major decisions, and both of them were happier.

Their relief may have stemmed from the fact that men experience risk and danger differently than women and are more tolerant of it, whereas women are generally more risk averse (Roszkowski 2010). In no way am I suggesting that men are superior at making decisions or that men should be in charge of money or business. But history and research are abundantly clear that men are more willing to embrace risk, danger, and the attending emotional discomfort. Hopefully I've sufficiently emphasized throughout the book that gender differences don't imply superiority on either side. For every man who is foolishly willing to risk his safety or fortune, there's a woman with common sense who would take a safer path.

Not every woman will want a relationship like Pete and Amy's, nor will every man. But if you wish to capitalize on a man's willingness to protect you and embrace discomfort on your behalf, there are plenty of us who will step up to the plate.

Some women appreciate that. When I asked women what they like about men, this was a common theme:

* "I like that men are daredevils at times and protective at other times."

* "I love the way their hugs feel, so strong and protective."

* "I don't need to be protected by a man, but I like that my man is willing to do it."

Forgiving and Forgetting

Most men have the ability to engage in a serious disagreement with another man then have a beer together as if nothing had happened. It's an ability that some women seem to admire:

* "I like that men are more forthright about their thoughts. I like that men can disagree with each other and that doesn't seriously endanger their relationships."

* "They seem to forgive and move on very easily."

* "I envy many of the abilities that seem innate to men, like the ability to not internalize. They forgive more quickly and easily."

Earlier in the book, I discussed the importance status and hierarchy hold for men, along with men's tendency to function well in large groups. Those qualities contribute to our readiness to forgive because life in a large group is easier when a person doesn't carry grudges. Within a large, loosely connected group, bearing a grudge has little benefit after order has been restored and questions of status have been settled.

There's evidence that men and women process forgiveness differently. Though we can be more vengeful than women when we hold a grudge, researchers have found that men indeed are quicker to forgive. Men are more responsive to what researchers call forgiveness prompts, such as recalling or being reminded that they've made similar mistakes in the past. Even simply raising the idea of forgiveness is a forgiveness prompt for men. And though it might seem counterintuitive, researchers found that men are more likely to engage in perspective taking, which creates empathy for a transgressor (Root and Exline 2011).

Of course, women are also forgiving, but the same researchers found that women tend to view forgiveness as a process that requires emotional healing. Men view forgiveness differently. We see it as a one-time decision rather than a lengthy procedure; we tend to forgive and then move on.

The mangineering approach to relationships recognizes that it's often more useful to forgive and forget. Maintaining a gunnysack full of past transgressions is bound to create destructive resentment—a dangerous element in the male social world.

The mind is reluctant to forget mistakes, injuries, and transgressions. However, it isn't necessary to follow the mind's impulse to focus or act on those thoughts. (For much more about disobeying the mind's impulses, you might read my previous book, *The User's Guide to the Human Mind*.)

The Joy of Simplicity

Men admire women's emotional depth. You might recall the man in chapter 9 who said, "I love the way women don't fear emotion. I love the way they live with open hearts." The other side of that emotional depth is simplicity—the willingness and ability to embrace the here and now without being drawn into the mind's stream of thoughts and feelings. Of course, sometimes men's simplicity is a source of frustration or bemusement for women. As one woman put it, "Can men really not be thinking about anything?"

I'll let some of the guys answer that question:

* "Women find it hard to believe that it's possible for a man to be thinking of nothing at all, but it's true. We do that."

* "When we say we're thinking about nothing, we are often truly thinking about nothing or are distracted by something

175

unrelated. Sometimes our minds are just wandering aimlessly."

* "Most of the time when we say we're thinking about nothing, we're really either thinking about nothing or thinking about something that has no real significance."

Perhaps this frustrates women because it seems like detachment. Here's one woman's observation: "Men can't keep track of relationship details at all. A typical example is when a male friend will tell me he ran into so-and-so at the supermarket. Then I ask him specific questions, and he can't answer any of them. Did she have her baby? 'I don't know.' Did he get that giant tattoo of the phoenix he was saving money for? 'I don't know.' Was her skin still yellow from the jaundice? 'I didn't notice.'"

Thinking about nothing might resemble inattentiveness. It might seem that relationships are unimportant to a man who fails to track details about people. But as one man explained to me, his romantic relationship was of vital importance even when it wasn't at the forefront of his mind.

If anything, the ability to soften our focus on a relationship and have a relaxed mind when we're with the women we love might indicate our comfort and confidence in the relationship. People generally covet the ability to escape anxiety and relax into an experience, and some women admire this quality in men:

* "What do I like most about men? Their simplicity—that sex and food can bring them happiness."

* "Men are easygoing and don't sweat the small stuff."

Complexity and simplicity: just one more way that women and men complement each other beautifully. Good relationship mangineering means making room for both.

Useful Stoicism

Let's revisit that old, false stereotype that men don't experience emotions as deeply as women. As I discussed earlier, men experience emotions as intensely as women, but they respond to emotions differently.

One group of researchers compared American women to relatively stoic Chinese men. They asked participants to view photos that were intended to elicit powerful negative emotions. Perhaps unsurprisingly, the women reported much higher levels of emotion than the men (Davis et al. 2012).

That's what the two groups *reported*. But apparently the situation was quite different behind the scenes. The researchers found that the men experienced negative emotions in response to the photos but quickly moved away from those feelings by engaging in emotional distancing strategies, whereas the women didn't.

The men used several strategies to manage the emotional discomfort: They avoided dwelling on the pictures. They distracted themselves by thinking of other things. They shifted their attention away from the unpleasant focal point of the pictures to more benign details. They also suppressed their emotional responses by controlling their facial expression, which helps contain emotional reactions.

So although men and women are quite similar emotionally, men seem to develop skills for distancing themselves from unpleasant feelings. (I believe we can partly credit that peewee football training I mentioned earlier, along with countless other childhood experiences.)

The researchers noted one more important detail: the female study participants tended to ruminate more about the causes of their emotional states than the men did. So while the men were moving away from their unpleasant emotional experiences, the women were focusing on them. That's not necessarily a bad thing. Contemplating the causes of an emotional state can be useful. It can help identify the source of relationship problems, for example.

Other times, however, it's more useful to focus away from the emotional aspect of an experience and get down to the business of pragmatic problem solving. That's where emotional distancing can be useful. This skill comes in handy when it's time to eliminate a big spider from the bathtub, snake the main sewer line, or do any of the other unpleasant tasks that men are usually willing to tackle. It's a skill that isn't lost on the women who made these observations:

* "I like that men are logical thinkers. That their world is usually black-and-white."

* "I find it comforting that men can dispassionately assess a situation."

* "Many times I want to hash out a problem without a lot of emotion. In general, men are better than I am at intellectual focus on an issue."

It's not that we're braver, that we don't experience emotions, or that we're more emotionally intelligent than women. In fact, you could argue that our habit of emotional distancing makes us less educated about our own emotions. Rather, it seems that we're well practiced at regulating our responses to emotions, whereas women are more skilled at understanding the sources of emotion. The skilled mangineer knows that both abilities are necessary and useful.

Goal Orientation

Some people feel compelled to understand where problems come from; others just want to know how to fix things. Of the couples who meet with me to sort out their relationship difficulties, it's often (though not always) the woman who feels compelled to dissect problems. Frequently the man simply wants to arrive at a solution and move on.

I may be starting to sound like a broken record, but both approaches are useful and necessary. Sometimes a couple

> ## How Men Think
>
> "**Women seem to focus more on the problem rather than the solution.**"

needs to identify why a problem happens, especially if it's a recurring problem. Other times it's more productive to find a solution and get on with life, especially if the problem was a one-time glitch.

It might seem strange to hear a psychologist say this, but in my experience, successful couples don't dissect every little problem they encounter. Instead, they prioritize and focus their attention on the important or repetitive issues. For example, while I was working with one couple, the wife inadvertently insulted her husband by appearing to question his effectiveness at his job. It was the kind of comment they could have spent days trying to deconstruct: *You say you didn't mean it, but a statement like that must reflect a subconscious disrespect for me. We need to talk about that.*

But the truth was, it was simply a poorly phrased expression of concern. So she clarified her meaning, he asked her to be more thoughtful about the topic in the future, and the rest of their day was fine. Problem solved.

Still, it's important to note that many women reported frustration with male goal-directedness, as these comments indicate:

* "Their desire to solve problems overshadows all attempts to communicate."

* "Men are way too goal oriented in bed. I want them to take their time. They want to go right for the gold."

Those women are correct that too much of a good thing can be bad. But many women do seem to value men's goal orientation when it's moderate, as these women attest:

* "The positive side of men being less talkative than women is that they're more likely to be direct about a problem."

* "I like men's straightforwardness and their focus on problem solving."

* "I actually love that men are doers, that they want to help you fix your problems and offer solutions. If I want to just gripe about something, I tell my partner up front. Otherwise it's nice to have a fresh perspective on solving a problem."

Each couple has to find their own balance between processing a problem and solving it—and that balance often shifts from situation to situation. The wise couple seeks that ongoing beer-and-pretzel balance. Here's one good man's advice on the subject: "Men are simpler creatures—goal oriented and logic driven. Sometimes we just don't get the emotional nuances. Be patient with us, and we'll try to be patient with you as well."

Playfulness

Remember the bowerbirds I mentioned in chapter 4? To attract the attention of hens, the male birds build clever displays on the forest floor that serve to showcase their fitness as mates, which is influenced by their intelligence. You might recall from the same chapter that humor is one of the ways men display intelligence and fitness in order to attract women. You like us more when we make you laugh.

Male bowerbirds don't maintain the bowers after they've finished mating. The little displays scatter with the wind, I suppose. But it's a different story with men. While we don't keep up the same intensity in our attempts to impress you as the relationship matures (you'd have to be a man to know how difficult that is), we do want to keep having a good time and making you laugh.

In my survey, this is one of the themes that men and women seemed to widely agree upon. Men want to relax and have fun with the women in their lives, and women reported that humor is one of the things they most admire in men. However, several men reported that they get frustrated because it often seems like their partners are unwilling to be playful. This comment captures that feeling: "Women can go on and on complaining and repeating, which is tiring. Why can't we talk about good stuff, relax, and enjoy our time together? I don't see how sharing negative emotions can deepen the relationship."

That man reflects a common sentiment, but I think he's missing something in the second part of his statement. Up to a point, sharing negative emotions can bring closeness. Still, his statement reflects a frustration that many men have shared with me: the women in their lives seem resistant to embracing the good moments in life.

I'm always a bit more optimistic about a couple's future when they've managed to maintain their playfulness through troubled times. Luckily, even when it's lost, playfulness is one of the easier assets to restore in a relationship, and good men are usually more than willing to lead the way. After all, we live to make you happy.

The Best of Both

I'd like to close this chapter with a little thought experiment. Suppose there were two islands, each with all of the amenities of modern life. On one island live ten thousand men and no women, and on the other, ten thousand women and no men. What do you suppose these societies would look like after a few decades?

My guess is that the men's island would be a lonely place—probably strewn with dirty socks. Sure, we'd have fun building racetracks and football stadiums, but we would be missing the most important part of our lives. We would lack purpose. And like men who avoid women in the real world, we would probably die earlier than we should (Kaplan and Kronick 2006).

As for the women's island, I can only guess that it would be comfortable but incomplete. Women might find that they miss our resourcefulness, our differing perspective, and our ability to make household items out of duct tape.

Decades of research have shown that marriage gives both men and women longer, happier lives. Married people are less likely to have pneumonia, cancer, or heart attacks, and they are also less likely to need surgery (Parker-Pope 2010). It's important to note that the quality of the relationship matters. A stressful marriage can be worse on a person's health than no marriage at all. In addition, recent research suggests that some of the benefits of married life apply equally well to committed cohabitation (Musick and Bumpass 2012). It all boils down to this: men and women are happier and healthier when we have each other.

Luckily, we don't live on separate islands. I think that's especially fortunate for men. And it isn't a bad deal for women either, as most of us men are pretty easy to live with if you know how we work. All we ask is acceptance, romance, and a bit of recognition. The only other thing a good man wants is to return the favor.

Epilogue

'd like to give the last word to the good men who anonymously and generously shared their thoughts as I was writing this book. What follows are a few of the comments I haven't yet included. Unfortunately, there isn't room for all of them.

I don't know much about the guys whose words appear here other than a few sparse facts: their ages ranged from seventeen to seventy, and they were thoughtful and articulate. Beyond that, I think it's safe to assume that they are good men doing the best they can in their relationships and in their lives.

Some of the men were clearly struggling with their relationships, but from the tone and content of their comments it seems safe to assume that few, if any, were struggling with the types of things that make a man ill prepared for a relationship. The depth and thoughtfulness of their responses are uncharacteristic of what you might hear from men trapped in struggles against problems such as addiction, incarceration, and violence.

It's important to keep in mind that my online survey was hardly scientific. The men and women who responded were self-selected. They all stumbled across the survey through similar channels, and they are probably of a similar stripe in some unquantified respect.

For what it's worth, I noticed a difference in tone between the women and men who expressed unhappiness with the opposite sex. More women expressed anger at men than vice versa, and the women's expressions of anger were generally more intense. For example, one woman wrote, "I'm not sure I like anything about men anymore, but I do live on the same planet so I'm at least polite, mostly."

While some men were pointed in their frustration about women, they more commonly expressed hopelessness and resignation. They sometimes expressed their frustration in a humorous way, like the man who wrote, "I understand everything about women except all those weird things they do." There were a few older men who indicated that they were trapped in marriages with wives who would never be happy, so they had given up trying. Their words conveyed a deep sadness.

The good news is that, on both sides, anger and hopelessness were vastly overshadowed by curiosity and admiration, even if tinged with a few frustrations. I'll start with some of the things men wish women understood about the male mind and save the best and most complimentary comments for last.

What Men Want Women to Know About Communication

One of my questions to men was "What do you wish women understood about the way men think or communicate?"

* "I think men are pretty simple creatures that women try to make more complicated. I know I'm generalizing, but I believe it's true. Men think in a line, and if there are too many inputs, we get confused. We need focus when talking."

* "Our style of communication is different from yours. We do our best to understand you, and for the most part we do

understand, even if it doesn't look like it. We don't always have the answers or know exactly the right way to respond, but we want to help you. Don't attack us when we're trying to help because that will make us less likely to care in the future."

* "I find that women tend to be coy regarding their desires. I can only guess so much. Sarcasm and passive-aggressive behavior tend to leave me confused and wondering what happened."

* "It may be true that women communicate more, but quantity doesn't guarantee quality. It would help if women were more straightforward about what they want and need. If you want me to just listen, then tell me straight. I will listen. If there's something serious you want to discuss with me, make sure to summarize and use direct language. Don't mind my feelings, I love you and I can handle the truth. And tell me to turn the TV off if you want to talk."

* "If you really want to know what we're thinking and you press us on it, don't be surprised if you don't like the answer. We were probably keeping it to ourselves because we knew you'd be hurt. It's probably not personal, though."

* "We aren't as skillful or as practiced with verbal stuff. How about some empathy? You think nothing of asking me to carry things, and I don't mind because I'm stronger and it makes me feel appreciated. But when we have an argument it's like I'm playing one-on-one against LeBron James. Why do you have to win every argument?"

* "What you see is what you get with men. A lot of misunderstandings are caused by women seeing men for what they want them to be, rather than what they really are."

* "Some of us aren't raised to be open with our feelings. Help us; don't judge us."

What Men Wish Women Understood

I also asked men, "What do you think women will never really understand about men?"

* "The quick response to female attractiveness, and the difficulty men can have in controlling their response."

* "Sex drive and personal ambition."

* "The power of female sexual attraction."

* "The constant desire for physical intimacy."

* "I don't think women will ever understand a man's sex drive. Testosterone is a merciless master."

* "I wish women understood a man's tendencies to break a situation down to its basic components and analyze everything before making a decision."

* "The role that honor plays in a man's life, including his working and personal relationships and his place in society."

* "I don't think women understand how we just let stuff roll off our backs and move on."

* "The worst moments are the time it takes for women to get okay again after a conflict. Sometimes it takes weeks, man!"

* "Women will never understand men's need to be silent once in a while. If they can't hear our words, they assume something is wrong. This isn't true, of course. Sometimes we just need a little time to ponder things and work them out in our heads before talking with our partners."

* "Our need to be alone, have our own way of doing things, and have our own personal identity."

* "I don't think they understand a man's need to occasionally be alone or in the company of other men."

Advice from Men to Women

I didn't ask men for relationship advice, but I should have. Several men offered useful thoughts. Here are a few:

* "Simplicity can really be an awesome thing!"

* "Sometimes silence is the best strategy."

* "If you want openness, don't punish it."

* "Don't pathologize our focus on something other than emotion."

* "Our testosterone all but blinds us to your faults. Your only real critics are other women. Stop overthinking."

* "All any man wants is to feel needed from time to time."

* "When you're negative about life, that only leads me to believe I should lighten your load and exclude myself from it."

* "Men need space periodically in order to grow closer. When a man pulls away for a time, it's not always or necessarily that you've done something wrong; he probably just needs to feel his own autonomy again. A man needs to be able to feel like himself, and just himself, from time to time in the process of getting closer to someone."

* "Men aren't meant to be like women. Feminism has convinced women that men should be just like them. It's not bad to be different."

* "Being demanding or entitled is unattractive because it eliminates the ability to be grateful and thankful. Men need to be thanked and encouraged for the things they do. Once a woman expects a man to just do things for her, then it's difficult for the man to keep doing those things no matter how much he loves her."

* "I'm happy and content to be in the same room with you. Our physical presence together is often enough to make me feel good. So I don't feel the need to 'connect' verbally as much as you do. I'm connected just sitting beside you."

What Men Love About Women

Finally, I asked men what they like most about women. The guys were quite forthcoming. It seems that we like you—a lot. Here is a short list of the reasons you consistently capture our hearts:

* "We males are often troublesome creatures, and women seem strangely willing to love us despite our flaws. I can never be too thankful for that."

* "I love how some women don't realize how beautiful and graceful they are. I love how, as men, we will never fully understand the mysterious creatures that women are, but I can't wait to spend my life trying to fully get to know just one."

* "I love that they can be so gentle in their touch, I love the feel of their bodies (in all shapes and sizes!), and I love when they talk about their feelings."

* "One of the best moments with any woman is the first time you reach out to hold her hand and she reaches out to hold yours."

* "Women need to understand that men would rather be around them than most anywhere."

* "The sight of certain women can make me forget my name. The only thing better than that is when the same women can converse on a variety of subjects."

* "I love almost everything about them!"

* "Their intelligence. An intelligent girl is worth the world and even more!"

* "The best non-bedroom-related moments are the simple ones, like shopping for food in an outdoor market, then going home and cooking and eating together. That's the life."

* "Their smell, soft skin, and tender touch. Sometimes when you look in their eyes you can see all the way to their soul."

* "I enjoy cuddling after sex. Surprisingly enough, guys like to just relax afterward. We might not hold you close or talk all the time, but it's nice to have you in the bed with us."

* "Their softness, both of body and spirit. It's alluring to see a woman who needs just a little help. I don't want an invalid, but I like to open the jars and the doors for her. It's a good feeling to see her smile because I could do something small for her."

* "The curves, smiles, eyes, laughter, softness, and tenderness. Seeking me for security and companionship, and the way they make my heart jump."

* "Introducing my wife to my family was one of the best days of my life."

* "Getting a hug and kiss the moment I walk in the door from work."

* "That they can make everything feel better with just a hug. That they have the power to make a man melt with just a smile."

* "The way they walk, talk, smell, and see the world and, of course, their bodies, no matter the shape."

* "Women are generally sweet, gentle, caring, thoughtful, and healthy, and the way they can seem so effortlessly graceful sometimes is utterly breathtaking."

* "The best moments are lying in bed going to sleep, when she lays her head on my shoulder and lets out a sigh. That tells me she feels happy and safe in my arms."

* "Without women, men would be lost. They give us the purpose we need to live honest and meaningful lives."

I cannot add a thing to that.

References

Baker, M. D., and J. K. Maner. 2008. "Risk-Taking as a Situationally Sensitive Male Mating Strategy." *Evolution and Human Behavior* 29:391–395.

Baumeister, R. 2010. *Is There Anything Good About Men? How Cultures Flourish by Exploiting Men.* New York: Oxford University Press.

Baur, N., and H. Hofmeister. 2008. "Some Like Them Hot: How Germans Construct Male Attractiveness." *Journal of Men's Studies* 16:280–300.

Benenson, J. F., and A. Heath. 2006. "Boys Withdraw More in One-on-One Interactions, Whereas Girls Withdraw More in Groups." *Developmental Psychology* 42:272–282.

Brody, S. 2010. "The Relative Health Benefits of Different Sexual Activities." *Journal of Sexual Medicine* 7:1336–1361.

Buss, D. M. 1998. "Sexual Strategies Theory: Historical Origins and Current Status." *Journal of Sex Research* 35:19–31.

Campbell, L., and B. J. Ellis. 2005. "Commitment, Love, and Mate Retention." In *The Handbook of Evolutionary Psychology*, edited by D. M. Buss. Hoboken, NJ: John Wiley and Sons.

Catsambis, S. 2005. "The Gender Gap in Mathematics." In *Gender Differences in Mathematics: An Integrative Psychological Approach*, edited by A. M. Gallagher and J. C. Kaufman. Cambridge, UK: Cambridge University Press.

Ceci, S. J., and W. M. Williams. 2010. "Sex Differences in Math-Intensive Fields." *Current Directions in Psychological Science* 19:275–279.

Clarke, J. N. 2009. "The Portrayal of Depression in Magazines Designed for Men." *International Journal of Men's Health* 8:202–212.

Coleman, D., M. S. Kaplan, and J. T. Casey. 2011. "The Social Nature of Male Suicide: A New Analytic Model." *International Journal of Men's Health* 10:240–252.

Davis, E., E. Greenberger, S. Charles, C. Chen, L. Zhao, and Q. Dong. 2012. "Emotion Experience and Regulation in China and the United States: How Do Culture and Gender Shape Emotion Responding?" *International Journal of Psychology* 47:230–239.

Deary, I. J., G. Thorpe, V. Wilson, J. M. Starr, and L. J. Whalley. 2003. "Population Sex Differences in IQ at Age 11: The Scottish Mental Survey 1932." *Intelligence* 31:533–542.

Dunn, M. J., and R. Searle. 2010. "Effects of Manipulated Prestige-Car Ownership on Both Sex Attractiveness Ratings." *British Journal of Psychology* 101:69–80.

Else-Quest, N., A. Higgins, C. Allison, and L. C. Morton. 2012. "Gender Differences in Self-Conscious Emotional Experience: A Meta-Analysis." *Psychological Bulletin* 5:947–981.

Fisher, T. D., Z. T. Moore, and M. Pittenger. 2012. "Sex on the Brain? An Examination of Frequency of Sexual Cognitions as a Function of Gender, Erotophilia, and Social Desirability." *Journal of Sex Research* 49:69–77.

Frankenhuis, W. E., and J. C. Karremans. 2012. "Uncommitted Men Match Their Risk Taking to Female Preferences, While Committed Men Do the Opposite." *Journal of Experimental Social Psychology* 48:428–431.

Gallup, G. G., R. L. Burch, and T. J. Berens Mitchell. 2006. "Semen Displacement as a Sperm Competition Strategy: Multiple Mating, Self-Semen Displacement, and Timing of In-Pair Copulations." *Human Nature* 17:253–264.

Gangestad, S. W., and R. Thornhill. 2003. "Facial Masculinity and Fluctuating Asymmetry." *Evolution and Human Behavior* 24:231–241.

Gangestad, S. W., R. Thornhill, and C. E. Garver-Apgar. 2010. "Men's Facial Masculinity Predicts Changes in Their Female Partners' Sexual Interests Across the Ovulatory Cycle, Whereas Men's Intelligence Does Not." *Evolution and Human Behavior* 31:412–424.

Garaigordobil, M. 2009. "A Comparative Analysis of Empathy in Childhood and Adolescence: Gender Differences and Associated Socio-emotional Variables." *International Journal of Psychology and Psychological Therapy* 9:217–235.

Giblin, P. 2011. "Men Making and Keeping Commitments." *American Journal of Family Therapy* 39:124–138.

Green, J. D., and M. E. Addis. 2012. "Individual Differences in Masculine Gender Socialization as Predictive of Men's Psychophysiological Responses to Negative Affect." *International Journal of Men's Health* 11:63–82.

Greengross, G., and G. Miller. 2011. "Humor Ability Reveals Intelligence, Predicts Mating Success, and Is Higher in Males." *Intelligence* 39:188–192.

Guéguen, N., and L. Lamy. 2012. "Men's Social Status and Attractiveness: Women's Receptivity to Men's Date Requests." *Swiss Journal of Psychology* 71:157–160.

Harskamp, E., N. Ding, and C. Suhre. 2008. "Group Composition and Its Effect on Female and Male Problem-Solving in Science Education." *Educational Research* 50:307–318.

Huoviala, P., and M. J. Rantala. 2013. "A Putative Human Pheromone, Androstadienone, Increases Cooperation Between Men." *PLoS ONE* 8(5):e62499.

Kaplan, R. M., and R. G. Kronick. 2006. "Marital Status and Longevity in the United States Population." *Journal of Epidemiology and Community Health* 60:760–765.

Keagy, J., J. F. Savard, and G. Borgia. 2009. "Male Satin Bowerbird Problem-Solving Ability Predicts Mating Success." *Animal Behavior* 78:809–817.

Kring, A. M., and A. H. Gordon. 1998. "Sex Differences in Emotion: Expression, Experience, and Physiology." *Journal of Personality and Social Psychology* 74:686–703.

Kuhn, S. L., and M. C. Stiner. 2006. "What's a Mother to Do?" *Current Anthropology* 47:953–980.

Lehrer, J. 2012. "Groupthink." *New Yorker*, Jan. 30, 22.

Li, N. P., V. Griskevicius, K. M. Durante, P. K. Jonason, D. J. Pasisz, and K. Aumer. 2009. "An Evolutionary Perspective on Humor: Sexual Selection or Interest Indication?" *Personality and Social Psychology Bulletin* 35:923–936.

Lin, W. L., K. Y. Hsu, H. C. Chen, and J. W. Wang. 2012. "The Relations of Gender and Personality Traits on Different Creativities: A Dual-Process Theory Account." *Psychology of Aesthetics, Creativity, and the Arts* 6:112–123.

Little, K. C., J. K. McNulty, and M. Russel. 2010. "Sex Buffers Intimates Against the Negative Implications of Attachment Insecurity." *Personality and Social Psychology Bulletin* 36:484–498.

McIntyre, M. H., A. Y. Li, J. F. Chapman, S. F. Lipson, and P. T. Ellison. 2011. "Social Status, Masculinity, and Testosterone in Young Men." *Personality and Individual Differences* 51:392–396.

Murdock, G. P. 1967. *Ethnographic Atlas.* Pittsburgh: University of Pittsburgh Press.

Musick, K., and L. Bumpass. 2012. "Reexamining the Case for Marriage: Union Formation and Changes in Well-Being." *Journal of Marriage and Family* 74:1–18.

Nummi, P., and J. Pellikka. 2012. "Do Female Sex Fantasies Reflect Adaptations for Sperm Competition?" *Annales Zoologici Fennici* 49:93–102.

Osborn, A. 1948. *Your Creative Power: How to Use Imagination.* New York: Charles Scribner's Sons.

Palmer, C. T., and C. F. Tilly. 1995. "Access to Females as a Motivation for Joining Gangs: An Evolutionary Approach." *Journal of Sex Research* 32:213–217.

Parker-Pope, T. 2010. "Is Marriage Good for Your Health?" *New York Times Magazine*, Apr. 18, 46.

Prokosch, M. D., R. G. Coss, J. E. Scheib, and S. A. Blozis. 2009. "Intelligence and Mate Choice: Intelligent Men Are Always Appealing." *Evolution and Human Behavior* 30:11–20.

Root, B. L., and J. J. Exline. 2011. "Gender Differences in Response to Experimental Forgiveness Prompts: Do Men Show Stronger Responses Than Women?" *Basic and Applied Social Psychology* 33:182–193.

Roszkowski, M. J. 2010. "Gender Differences in Personal Income and Financial Risk Tolerance: How Much of a Connection?" *Career Development Quarterly* 58:270–275.

Schmitt, D. P. 2005. "Fundamentals of Human Mating Strategies." In *The Handbook of Evolutionary Psychology*, edited by D. M. Buss. Hoboken, NJ: John Wiley and Sons.

Schmitt, D. P., and 118 members of the International Sexuality Description Project. 2003. "Universal Sex Differences in the Desire for Sexual Variety: Tests from 52 Nations, 6 Continents, and 13 Islands." *Journal of Personality and Social Psychology* 85:85–104.

Shackelford, T. K., D. P. Schmitt, and D. M. Buss. 2005. "Universal Dimensions of Human Mate Preferences." *Personality and Individual Differences* 39:447–458.

Simon, R. W., and A. E. Barrett. 2010. "Nonmarital Romantic Relationships and Mental Health in Early Adulthood: Does the Association Differ for Women and Men?" *Journal of Health and Social Behavior* 51:168–182.

Smith, A., J. Ferris, J. Richters, M. Pitts, J. Shelley, and J. M. Simpson. 2011. "Sexual and Relationship Satisfaction Among Heterosexual Men and Women: The Importance of Desired Frequency of Sex." *Journal of Sex and Marital Therapy* 37:104–115.

Smith, S. 2011. *The User's Guide to the Human Mind: Why Our Brains Make Us Unhappy, Anxious, and Neurotic and What We Can Do About It.* Oakland, CA: New Harbinger.

Starratt, V. G., and T. K. Shackelford. 2012. "He Said, She Said: Men's Reports of Mate Value and Mate Retention Behaviors in Intimate Relationships." *Personality and Individual Differences* 53:459–462.

Stenstrom, E., G. Saad, M. V. Nepomuceno, and Z. Mendenhall. 2011. "Testosterone and Domain-Specific Risk: Digit Ratios (2D:4D and Rel2) as Predictors of Recreational, Financial, and Social Risk-Taking Behaviors." *Personality and Individual Differences* 51:412–416.

Taylor, D. W., P. C. Berry, and C. H. Block. 1958. "Does Group Participation When Using Brainstorming Facilitate or Inhibit Creative Thinking?" *Administrative Science Quarterly* 3:23–47.

Tovée, M. J., and P. L. Cornelissen. 2001. "Female and Male Perceptions of Female Physical Attractiveness in Front-View and Profile." *British Journal of Psychology* 92:391–402.

Van Vugt, M., D. De Cremer, and D. P. Janssen. 2007. "Gender Differences in Cooperation and Competition: The Male Warrior Hypothesis." *Psychological Science* 18:19–23.

Watkins, C. D., and B. C. Jones. 2012. "Priming Men with Different Contest Outcomes Modulates Their Dominance Perceptions." *Behavioral Ecology* 23:539–543.

Wegner, D. M., D. J. Schneider, S. R. Carter, and T. L. White. 1987. "Paradoxical Effects of Thought Suppression." *Journal of Personality and Social Psychology* 53(1):5–13.

Wilbur, C. J., and L. Campbell. 2011. "Humor in Romantic Contexts: Do Men Participate and Women Evaluate?" *Personality and Social Psychology Bulletin* 37:918–929.

Wilder, J. A., Z. Mobasher, and M. F. Hammer. 2004. "Genetic Evidence for Unequal Effective Population Sizes of Human Females and Males." *Molecular Biology and Evolution* 21:2047–2057.

Wilson, M., and M. Daly. 1985. "Competitiveness, Risk Taking, and Violence: The Young Male Syndrome." *Ethnology and Sociobiology* 6:59–73.

Shawn T. Smith, PsyD, is a psychologist in private practice in Denver, CO. He is author of the book *The User's Guide to the Human Mind,* and writes a blog at ironshrink.com. Smith enjoys various manly activities, including being a husband and father. He lives with his wife and daughter, and their dog.

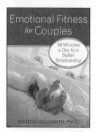
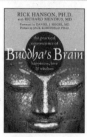
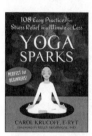